EXIT STRATEGY

GOD'S PLAN TO BRING HIS CHILDREN HOME

Dr. Rob Tibbitts

Published by
Innovo Publishing, LLC
www.innovopublishing.com
1-888-546-2111

Providing Full-Service Publishing Services for
Christian Authors, Artists & Organizations: Hardbacks, Paperbacks,
eBooks, Audiobooks, Music & Videos

Exit Strategy
God's Plan to Bring His Children Home

ISBN 13: 978-1-936076-87-1
ISBN 10: 1-936076-87-X

Cover Design & Interior Layout: Innovo Publishing, LLC

Printed in the United States of America
U.S. Printing History

Second Edition: July 2011

To My Commander in Chief
(Dedication)

For me, writing this book has been a lot like bringing a child into the world. Years of intimate fellowship with God inevitably led me to the moment of conception when God started something inside of me that I knew I had to see through to completion—or forever live with the haunting question of "What if?" Conception was followed by long days, and short nights of gestation and anticipation as the project grew, took shape, and developed a heartbeat of its own.

As the great day of its delivery rapidly approached, a new wave of emotions flooded my mind. Suddenly it occurred to me—this little piece of me is about to be thrust into the world for all to see. Questions of doubt caused me to ask, "What was I thinking when I agreed to bring this child into the world?" The only thing that caused me to push through the hours of labor pains needed to give birth to this project was the belief that what I had nurtured for all these months was conceived by God and bore His image, even if that image is somehow marred by my own DNA.

Having said all of that, I present to you my firstborn! Any good contained in the pages of this book comes from God's side of the family, and any and all deficiencies come from my side of the family. I pray that God will use this book, in spite of its shortcomings, to make an impact in this world. I hope you will be kind to my "child"; after all, he did not choose to be born!

With these things in mind, I wholeheartedly dedicate this book to the One in whom I find my being: the Only True God. May I be found passionately pursuing, faithfully following, and single-heartedly serving Him when I draw my final breath.

THANKS TO THE TROOPS
(Acknowledgments)

I feel like an actor at an awards show who has so many people to thank but only so much time in which to do so. My family has sacrificed much to make this book a reality. My incredible wife, Janet, believed in me when I did not believe in myself. She has read and re-read this manuscript so many times—improving it each and every time. Thanks Sweetheart! My three children, Katherine, Ryan, and Rebecca have done without me many nights as I have retreated to write yet another chapter. Thanks guys—you're about to get Dad back!

My all-time favorite military hero, Major Timothy Neal Bible, Psychological Operations Officer, has helped me with so many of the military terms and concepts in the development of this manuscript. Thanks, Neal, for the help, and for the freedom that you provide me and mine!

My extended family and close friends have pitched in financially to help underwrite the cost of publication. They not only believed in what I was doing, but they dug deep to make it possible. Thanks for your sacrifice so others can hear!

I would not be the person I am today if it were not for my godly parents, Bob and Letha. They lived out their faith as my brothers and I looked on. They laid the foundation others have built upon. Thanks Mom and Dad! No child could ask for more than you have given to me!

A group of my closest friends with whom I meet for Bible study each week contributed to this book in ways that are immeasurable. It was this incredible group of friends that kept asking me to teach them the book of Revelation. I put them off as long as I could, but they would not relent. It was during the preparation of those lessons that I made the life-changing discovery that eventually led to this book. I am so grateful to them for their persistence. Charles, Ann, Irma, Don, Chuck, Tee, Lori, Ruben, Lynn, Brenda, Mable, Tim, Diane, Becky, Denise, and Pauline, you are each an incredible blessing to my life. Thanks to each of you for the encouragement, the prayers, and the occasional spur in the backside ☺. We finally made it!

I also must thank the rest of my Crossroads family! You guys are the most wonderful people in the world. For almost two decades, you have allowed me the privilege of serving alongside you. You deserve a much better pastor, but I am eternally grateful that you settled for me! I love you with all of my heart. Thanks for allowing me to be me . . . and loving me anyway! I could not ask for a better family!

And finally, I must thank my new friends at Innovo Publishing. Bart and Terry have been so patient, encouraging, and helpful every single step of the way. Yvonne, you are an incredibly gifted graphic designer. Thanks for the best book cover ever! Darya, thanks for using your editing knowledge to identify my mistakes and improve my manuscript. You guys have a heart for the Lord and it shows in all that you do. Your team makes me look better than I really am. Thanks!

FAIR WARNING

(Preface)

Thanks for picking up this book. I hope that it will be a book you will have a hard time putting down. As the author, I believe I should share something with you right up front. Just as I am a work in progress, so is this book. While I am offering you the very best I have at this particular moment in time, I would assume—in fact, I would hope—that God is not finished teaching and maturing me yet. I do not pretend to have all the answers concerning the second coming of Christ, but I offer you the pieces of the puzzle that I have been able to put together so far.

The most difficult thing I have had to come to grips with is the fact that sooner or later every author must let go of his manuscript knowing full well that as soon as he does, he will make another discovery that could have been included. If you meet me a year from now, I would hope that my understanding of the second coming would be a little more advanced than it is right now. Having said that, I am sure I will need to fine tune parts of this book over time. It is not that God's Word will have changed, but hopefully my level of understanding will have increased.

I hope God will use this book to help you prepare yourself (and others) for the most incredible day of your life—the day you meet Jesus face to face. Hold this book in one hand and your Bible in the other. Compare what I share with you to the Word of God. If at any point you find that I have departed from God's Word, please forgive me, and by all means cling to the Word of God. His words are life! Mine are just a humble attempt to communicate His.

Road Map

(Contents)

ROAD MAP

(Contents)

INTRODUCTION:
REAL MEN DON'T NEED MAPS

One of my favorite places to vacation is Colorado. I love to go there in the winter because I love to snow ski. As a teenager on my first ski trip, I was determined to conquer the mountain. Ski lessons were included in my travel package, but I thought, "Lessons are for those who cannot figure this out on their own." I skipped the lessons, snapped on my skis, and worked my way over to the ski lift.

Working my way through the line at the ski-lift entrance proved tricky enough for me. I wasn't used to having five-foot-long boards attached to my boots. Each time I fell to the snow I noticed the people around me making more room for me to fall without taking them down with me. It is hard to look cool when you can't even make it through the ski-lift line without falling down several times. For some reason, the workers at the ski-lift entrance expect you to ski well enough to go five feet without falling. Everything seems high in Colorado including their expectations! After getting mowed down by the ski-lift bench, I was thankful for the emergency shut-off switch that stopped the whole lift long enough for me to get on board. After climbing aboard, I was soon headed somewhere high upon the mountain.

Halfway up the mountain it dawned on me that I did not have a clue where, or how I was going to exit the ski lift. You could say that in my eagerness to conquer the mountain, I had failed to develop an exit strategy! Not knowing what to expect, I had failed to prepare myself.

As the lift ascended high above the mountain, I noticed two things: all the lift chairs headed back down the mountain were empty, and I was way too high off the ground to jump out of my seat. I knew I did not have long to develop my exit strategy. I had to think fast! In a moment of sheer genius (okay it was more like deep desperation), I decided to watch the people ahead of me and then do what they did. It sounded like a great plan, but there was only one small problem: they obviously knew what they were doing, and I did not! They made it look so simple. It was not! They approached the landing, grabbed their poles, stood up, and skied off. I did not! My strategy was obviously flawed. Plan or no plan, I was not prepared when I reached the exit point. How unprepared was I? Let's just say I was glad they had another emergency shut-off switch at the ski-lift exit. By the way, if you have ever wondered whether or not those switches work, they do! I tested them several times that day.

After exiting the lift (that is a nice way of describing my clumsy dismount), reattaching my skis, and brushing the snow off my goggles and my face, I ran into a guy who had never skied before. When I say I ran into him, I mean I literally ran into him. Once we untangled our skis, we started down the mountain together. The funny thing about going down a snow-covered hill with long, skinny skis attached to your feet is that you can build up speed fast. I did not know anything about forming a "snow plow" with my skis or how to traverse the mountain from side to side to control my speed.

Since I skipped the lessons, I assumed we were supposed to head straight down the mountain; after all, that is what I had watched the skiers do in the Olympics. I figured all those people going slowly from side to side simply did not know how to ski. I can remember alerting those in front of me that I was "coming through" and that they had better beware. As I passed up one man at a high rate of speed I remember asking him, "How do you stop these things?" He yelled back, "Just fall backwards into the snow!" So, I took his advice—a lot that day—not always on purpose, and not always with grace!

On our fourth or fifth trip up the mountain, my new friend and I decided to get on a different lift; after all, the first ski-lift operator must have been tired of shutting the lift down every time we came through. There was only one problem; no one told us that different lifts went to different places on the mountain. They must have covered that in the lessons I decided to skip.

The new lift went to the "expert" section of the mountain. I promise you, there were no little "beginner slopes" on that part of the mountain—only one small cliff followed by another. Okay, they were not really cliffs, but they sure seemed like cliffs to me! I knew right then I was in trouble. There was no way I had the skills needed to get back to the bottom of the mountain. I thought I was going to die, so I started looking for a burial plot. Then it hit me; maybe all those "bumps on the hills" were where others had unsuccessfully tried to make it down the mountain, fallen, broken a bone, and then had lain there while fresh snow covered them up. I was determined not to die on that mountain, so I did what all good beginner skiers would do. I pleaded earnestly for God's help, took off my skis, and slid all the way down the mountain on my bottom. Thank God for thermal underwear!

Can you guess where I headed next? No, not the first-aid station . . . the map station! All of the sudden, possessing a map seemed like the wisest thing I could do. I not only picked up one map, I grabbed two just in case the first one was jarred loose on my next hard fall. Then, I did something that most guys would never admit to doing . . . I actually opened the map and studied it. I learned that each trail had been rated according to its level of difficulty—green, blue, and black. I also secretly wished that I had taken those lessons, which had long since ended. Had I taken the lessons, I would have been much better equipped to enjoy my very first ski trip, and the white parts of my body would have remained white instead of turning black and blue. In those lessons, the instructor would have shown me how to use my skis as a "snow plow" in order to control my speed, how to enter and exit the ski lift without the use of the emergency shut-off switch, and how to read the map of the mountain to ensure I did not end up in places never intended for a novice like me.

Since that first trip, I have made many more trips to the mountains of Colorado. Each trip supplies new memories that I will cherish for a lifetime. I have also introduced my children to the sport of snow skiing, but instead of turning them loose to repeat my mistakes, I gave them a map, escorted them up the mountain, and taught them how to make it back to the bottom safely. I hope this book will serve a similar purpose in your life as you seek to navigate the mountain of material related to the second coming of Christ.

The Bible makes it clear that all of human history is moving rapidly toward a very dramatic conclusion. In planning for that day, God has put in place an "exit strategy" for all who belong to Him. His followers are not called to devise their own exit strategies, but to get familiar with His exit strategy. Just as the ski lessons would have taught me how the architects of the ski slopes had intended for me to maximize my experience on their mountain, so God's Word teaches us how to prepare ourselves for His return. The more we understand what God's Word teaches, the more prepared and less anxious we will be as we approach that day.

As we begin this journey together, you should know that I am a visual person. I love to use metaphors to paint pictures that others can visualize. Perhaps that is why I love the way Jesus, Paul, and John use pictures and stories to tell us of the events of the end. I also like to take complex things and boil them down into bite-size pieces that are easy to digest. It has been said that lawyers take the simple things of life and complicate them, while communicators take the complicated things of life and simplify them. I am called by God to be a communicator! I hope my writing style proves that to be true.

Eighteen years ago when I preached my first message at the church I am privileged to serve, one of the members told me that I "hid my education well." Now, either he meant I sounded really stupid, or that I had preached my message using words and images to which he could relate. The curiosity was killing me. I had to know which he meant. As I inquired, he laughed and said that he really enjoyed the simple way I taught. I did not set out to be simple; it is just the way I process life. I think that is the way God intends for His Word to be—simple, straightforward, and understandable. We sometimes make it sound more complicated than God intended it to be.

It is my belief that true followers of Christ want to know how to prepare themselves for the return of Christ. No Christ-follower wants to be caught unprepared. It is for those individuals that I have written this book. My goal is not to impress you with big words or some "superior" knowledge (as if somehow I could), but instead, to prepare you for your exit from life's grand stage, whether through physical death or through the amazing return of Christ. We cannot improve on the exit strategy God has put in place for each of us, but we can adjust our lives and determine to live with the assurance that Christ is coming soon.

In this book, I am going to present you with a "map" of the mountain of material that the Bible provides related to the second coming of Christ. I have modeled my map after the one that Jesus presented to His disciples. Many curious students of the end make the same type of mistake I made on my first ski trip. They bypass the lessons of Christ and head straight for the mountain of material found in the rest of the Bible. When someone makes that mistake it is easy for them to become overwhelmed and end up in a place Christ never intended. Since Christ has provided us a map of the mountain, we would be wise to begin with what He has shared and allow the other biblical writers to color within His lines. Beginning this journey by exploring the exit strategy which Christ presented to His disciples, will prove critical, as well as foundational, to the development of a correct understanding of the rest of the Bible's teachings on the second coming of Christ.

I will not pretend to have all of the answers. In fact, there will be places where I will honestly admit that I am not sure how to interpret certain passages. I apologize for that in advance, but I feel it is better to admit my limitations than to try to fake you out (or lead you in the wrong direction). I am not asking you to blindly accept what I have written, but instead, to take the map that I offer and compare it to the teachings of the Bible. Only after close examination will you be able to determine for yourself if what I have written is true. If you find it to be accurate, as I hope you will, I would be honored if you would use my map as your own, and share it with others who will come behind you.

Please understand that my purpose is not to malign those who disagree with my conclusions. I am sure they are as sincere in their beliefs as I am in mine. We simply disagree! In my mind, that does not make us enemies; it simply reveals the limitations imposed upon us while we are confined to these mortal bodies. For now, as Paul reminds us, *"we see but a poor reflection as in a mirror; then we shall see face to face. Now I know in part; then I shall know fully, even as I am fully known"* (1 Cor. 13:12).

I willingly admit that much of what I will share with you has been influenced by many great biblical scholars. (I will list these resources in the back of this book for you to explore as you desire.) None of us live or learn in a vacuum. Men and women with far greater minds than mine have debated these issues for two thousand years. I have benefited greatly from researching their positions as I have pieced together the map I am about to present to you. To be very honest, in formulating my current beliefs I have benefited as much from the writings of those with whom I disagree as I did from those with whom I agree. Both sets of arguments caused me to reexamine Scripture to see for myself what God's Word revealed. Perhaps God will use this book in much the same way in your life.

SECTION ONE:

INTERNAL CONFLICT

As you are most certainly aware, there are almost as many theories concerning the second coming of Christ as there are authors. You may be asking yourself, "With all of the different theories in print today, how can one know for certain which is true?" That is a great question that needs to be addressed before we go any farther.

As Christians, we hold the firm conviction that the Word of God is Truth without any mixture of error. In other words, it is trustworthy in all that it reports. So, for a theory of the second coming of Christ to be considered true, it must be in agreement with the Word of God. Anything that disagrees with the Bible should be considered false and quickly discarded.

Even with that bedrock principle having been settled, there are some major disagreements within the Christian family concerning the correct way to interpret many of the passages that deal with the second coming of Christ. So, how can you know ***for certain*** which view of the second coming is accurate? The only way we can know something is completely accurate is when it perfectly aligns itself with Scripture. If at any point it does not align with Scripture, at least that portion of the theory must be set aside.

This principle looks great on paper. It is easy to write, and it is easy to preach, but it is much more difficult to implement. We seem to prefer clinging to what we have always believed instead of allowing those beliefs to be challenged by the truth of God's Word. We prefer comfort over change most days of the week. As a result, if we are not careful, we will come to Scripture to find support for what we have always believed instead of allowing the Holy Spirit to use Scripture to lead us into His truth (Jn. 16:13). While that is not easy to hear, it is our reality many times.

In this section, I wish to pull back the curtain and reveal my personal struggle to allow God's Word to dictate what I believed concerning the second coming of Christ. It was a struggle that shook me to my very core. I will also share with you what I previously held to be true and why I no longer believe those things to be true. I pray that God will use my story to help you evaluate what you believe, and why you believe it.

CHAPTER ONE
POINT OF NO RETURN

I am a changed man because of what I am about to share with you. I did not set out on this journey with the intention of having my beliefs changed, but when confronted with the things I am about to reveal to you, I was left with no other option but to change.

The information I am about to share with you might cause you to reexamine what you have been taught concerning the second coming of Christ. It certainly challenged some of my lifelong beliefs. While an experience of this sort is never comfortable, it is greatly beneficial for those who have committed themselves to building their lives on the truth of God's Word.

Almost without exception, those who have heard me explain the discoveries revealed in the remainder of this book were initially skeptical to embrace what I had to say. That is totally understandable. So was I! I asked my hearers to examine the Bible and see if my teachings were in alignment with Scripture. Their willingness to do so was exciting to me because I knew that by the time they had finished their investigation, their beliefs would rest upon the solid foundation of God's Word, and not just another man's opinion. I would love for you to take this same approach.

As I began preparing to lead my church family through a study on the end-times, I made the deliberate decision to allow the Bible to dictate where I came down on this highly debated, much-disputed subject. As a church family, we have committed ourselves to allow God's Word to be the final authority for our beliefs. When our beliefs are in alignment with God's Word, great! When they are not, we have agreed to adjust our beliefs to line up with Scripture. It is much more important for us to be "biblical" than to cling to an unbiblical tradition handed down to us.

In my studies of the events of the end-times, I began to discover things in God's Word that seemed to contradict what I had been taught all of my life. Initially, I was skeptical of my new conclusions. So, I frantically searched throughout the Bible to see if I could find other passages that would somehow reinforce my lifelong beliefs. I was unsuccessful.

Lacking the support I longed for in the Scriptures, I scoured through the writings of the "experts" who held the view I had been taught. I wanted to see if there was something I was missing in the Bible. Instead of their "explanations" clearing things up for me, they actually exposed even more gaping holes in their theories. I was amazed to learn that many of their theories were built around scriptures that had been taken completely out of context.

The more I read in the Bible, the more convinced I was that I had to change my beliefs in order to bring them in alignment with Scripture. That was a scary thing for me to do, but it was the right decision!

During this process, I felt myself growing a little angry. Mainly, I was angry at myself for believing something without first confirming it in Scripture. Over the years my teachers had all seemed to imply that the topic of the end-times was too difficult for the average person to understand. As a result, I invested my time and focused my studies on other portions of Scripture that were more on "my level." In doing so, I simply relied on other people's writings to shape my view of the end-times without investigating their claims for myself. Big mistake!

It was not long before the excitement of discovering how straightforwardly the Bible addressed the issue of the second coming chased those other emotions away. This topic was not nearly as complicated as I had been led to believe. My excitement about the things I was learning led to a sense of obligation to share these discoveries with those I love.

I soon learned that most of my discoveries were not unique to me. As I began to compare what I was uncovering in the Bible with what others had written long ago, I was amazed to learn how similar my new discoveries were to the writings of old. Many of the truths that God was revealing to me were the very things that those in the early Church had embraced. So, in essence, I was not stating brand-new discoveries, but instead, taking what the early Church believed and taught and putting it into a language people in our day could understand.

In this journey, you may experience some of the same emotions I felt. Please do not allow them to drive you away from the incredibly important message contained in this book. On several occasions in my life, I have discovered that in order for me to be willing to change, God had to first make me uncomfortable where I was. You may experience those feelings of discomfort in the next few pages. Please do not bail out. If change is necessary, allow God's Word to dictate those changes. You will never regret making that decision. As one man said: "To say I was mistaken is simply to admit that I am smarter now than I used to be."

Please, do not blindly accept what I am about to present to you. Instead, compare it with Scripture, and accept it, or reject it, based on those merits alone. I could not ask any more from you!

So, you may be asking yourself, "What was this guy taught that he later discovered to be inaccurate?" That is a great question. Allow me to quickly summarize what I had been taught concerning the return of Christ. Please understand that those who passed these things on to me were godly men who loved the Lord deeply. I do not doubt that for one minute. They were simply passing on to me what had been passed on to them.

My entire life I was taught that one day Christ would return on the clouds to resurrect the dead in Christ and to gather up the believers who were still alive on earth. This event was referred to as the "rapture." Both groups of Christians (dead and alive) would meet Christ in the air, where their lives would be evaluated, and their deeds would be rewarded. Because they had believed in Christ prior to His return, they would be allowed to skip the seven years of tribulation that were going to come upon the rest of those living on the earth. Instead of suffering through the tribulation, they would enjoy a huge celebration in Heaven known as the marriage supper of the Lamb.

Those who still lacked a relationship with Christ when He returned would be "left behind" to endure seven years of terrible tribulation while Satan ruled on the earth through the antichrist. Those who mistakenly thought they were Christians, but were not, would be granted other opportunities during the tribulation to repent and be saved. However, one of the consequences of not being saved prior to Christ's return is that they would have to go through the terrible trials associated with the tribulation.

The Jews would rebuild the temple in Jerusalem and reestablish the sacrificial system. During this time, the antichrist would gradually increase in fame and power, until he declared himself to be "god" at an event known as the Abomination of Desolation near the middle of the tribulation period.

I was taught that as these seven years of tribulation progressed, things would grow increasingly difficult for those who chose to follow Christ. During this period, the hearts and minds of the Jews would be opened to understand that Christ was the Messiah, and many Jews would be saved. They would then serve as God's missionaries to reach large numbers of people throughout the world. However, the new believers would be forced to face horrible deaths if they refused to take the mark of the beast as required by the antichrist and the false prophet.

At the end of the seven years of tribulation, Christ would return to earth with His saints for a battle known as Armageddon, which Christ was sure to win. The false prophet and the antichrist would be cast into Hell. Christ would reign with His saints on the earth for a thousand years while Satan was chained and cast into the bottomless pit. After the thousand-year reign, Satan would be released for a short time for one more battle before he would be cast eternally into the lake of fire where he would join the antichrist and the false prophet. Then, the Great White Throne Judgment would occur, and eternity would begin with the arrival of a new heaven and a new earth.

I was also taught that the main message of the book of Revelation pertained primarily to the Jews who would come to faith during the tribulation. Proponents of this theory claimed that the main message of Revelation was not intended for the Church, since the Church was not specifically mentioned after the third chapter of Revelation.

I was left with the impression that while the message of the book of Revelation was interesting, it was not something I needed to be too concerned about. After all, I would not be around to see any of the events unfold. I was taught that Christians should take great comfort in knowing they would not be required to suffer through the tribulation because God loves His children too much to allow them to live through such terrible trials. Believing these things to be true, I never invested the time and energy required to do a full investigation of the Bible's teachings concerning the end-times.

Does all of this sound familiar to you? Is this what you were taught would happen near the end? This particular view of the rapture has come to be known as the pretribulation view ("pre" signifying that the Church would be removed from the earth prior to the tribulation). It is very closely intertwined with another theory known as dispensationalism, which insists on maintaining a very clear distinction between God's dealings with the Jewish nation and His dealings with the New Testament Church.

If this is what you have been taught, you really should read the rest of this book. I hope that you will carefully consider what I am about to share with you. It very well could be the thing you need to hear in order to ensure that you are fully prepared for Christ's return.

The theory that I have outlined above is believable. I believed it for years, but that does not make it biblical. Everything in my flesh would like to believe that I will get to skip the terrible events of the final days, but just because thoughts like this are comforting to me, does not make them correct. Simply because a particular view is "popular" does not make it true. The thing that makes something biblical is that it is in alignment with the teachings of the Bible. The main problem with the dispensational pretribulation theory is that it lacks biblical support in many different areas.

Allow me to explain some of the main reasons why I no longer believe the theory I have presented above.

It Gives False Hope of a Second Chance

It clearly contradicts what Christ taught concerning the need for us to be prepared for His return. Their theory teaches that those who are not "saved" when He returns will be given further opportunities to repent and be saved during the tribulation following Christ's return. This is something that the teachings of Christ clearly deny (Mt. 25:1–46). While there will be individuals saved during the final days prior to Christ's return, once Christ has returned the Bible teaches that the window of opportunity for repentance and salvation will be closed. This will be explained in greater detail later in this book (See Section Two).

It Requires Multiple Raptures

While the term "rapture" is not specifically mentioned in the Bible, the concept of the rapture is very clearly spelled out. Paul wrote about that event in 1 Thessalonians 4:15–18 with these words:

> *For this we say to you by the word of the Lord, that we who are alive and remain until the coming of the Lord, will not precede those who have fallen asleep. For the Lord Himself will descend from heaven with a shout, with the voice of the archangel and with the trumpet of God, and the dead in Christ will rise first. Then we who are alive and remain will be caught up together with them in the clouds to meet the Lord in the air, and so we shall always be with the Lord. Therefore comfort one another with these words.*

In this passage, Paul mentions one event composed of two parts. The resurrection of those who have died in Christ will be immediately followed by the gathering up of believers who are still alive on the earth. Both groups will meet Christ in the air and remain with Him forever.

The dispensational pretribulation view requires multiple raptures. Some of its proponents claim there will be two raptures while others insist on even more. However, the Bible presents the rapture as a single event in history. Nowhere in the Bible is there found support for multiple raptures. Passages of Scripture have been taken out of context and twisted to imply that there will be multiple raptures. However, that is not what the Bible teaches.

Those who teach the multiple rapture theory claim that the first rapture (immediately before the tribulation) will occur "secretly," while the second rapture will be visible for all to see. This is also in contradiction to Christ's teaching where He says that all will see Him coming on the clouds. Jesus clearly stated, *"For just as the lightning comes from the east and flashes even to the west, so will the coming of the Son of Man be"* (Mt. 24:27). Supporters of the multiple rapture theory claim that the whole world will not see Him until

His "second" second coming at the conclusion of the tribulation. Some in this group insert a second rapture at the end of the tribulation (others go as far as to include three raptures) to gather up all of those who have come to faith in Christ during the seven years of the tribulation. Again, support for this cannot be found in Scripture without manipulating the text to say something it was never intended to say.

It Is Built Upon a Missing Passage

Supporters of the pretribulation view of the rapture also claim that John intended for the rapture to occur somewhere after the end of chapter three, and before the beginning of chapter four in the book of Revelation. Did you catch that? They claim that it mysteriously occurs in the blank space between chapters three and four. However, there is absolutely nothing that even closely resembles the rapture mentioned anywhere near that portion of Scripture. They agree that the Bible does not specifically mention the rapture at that point in time, but still, they insist that the Church must be raptured at that point because they cannot find the term "church" specifically mentioned anywhere after the third chapter of Revelation. They are simply wrong on both accounts.

First, the Church will not be raptured prior to the tribulation. That event will occur later in God's timeline. Jesus, Paul, and John all three place its timing late into the period of tribulation.

Second, the book of Revelation was written to inform the Church of the things that were yet to happen. The Church is addressed throughout the book of Revelation. The first three chapters contain warnings for seven churches that existed in John's day. The remainder of the book contains warnings for the Church that was to follow. John confirmed this when he wrote: *"Write, therefore, what you have seen, what is now and what will take place later"* (Rev. 1:19). He also reported being told in chapter four, *"Come up here, and I will show you what must take place after this"* (Rev. 4:1).

Claiming that the Church is not mentioned again in the book of Revelation is similar to claiming that the "Trinity" or the "rapture" is nowhere mentioned in Scripture. While neither of these two words (Trinity or rapture) is used in Scripture, both the Trinity and the rapture are clearly biblical concepts. Simply because they cannot find the term "church" used in the later parts of Revelation, does not mean that the Church was mysteriously removed after chapter three. It is obviously present throughout the remainder of the book.

It is my understanding that the entire book of Revelation was written to prepare the Church, which is made up of both Jews and Gentiles, for the turbulent times that await it. It also makes no sense to me that an event as significant as the rapture would be accidentally omitted from this portion of John's detailed chronology of end-time events. Why would John outline in such detail all the other events of the end, and then fail to mention the rapture? The rapture is a huge event. It is the thing that the Church has longed for since the first coming of Christ. To insinuate that John somehow would omit such an event is ludicrous. To further complicate their argument, one must remember that John was not acting alone as he recorded what he was shown. He was working under the inspiration of the Holy Spirit. So any "omission" would have to be attributed to the Holy Spirit as well as to John. I don't imagine that anyone committed to the authority of Scripture is ready to make such a claim.

How can serious students of the Bible, who claim to be committed to a literal interpretation of the Bible, proceed to build their end-time theory around a "passage of Scripture" that does not exist? Again, I don't mean to be antagonistic, but when I discovered that the theory, which had been handed down to me, was built around a mysteriously missing passage, I was astonished.

They Place the Rapture Before the Final Abomination of Desolation

Another major reason I no longer hold to the pretribulational view of the rapture has to do with an event the Bible calls the Abomination of Desolation. The Old Testament prophet, Daniel, referred in three different places to an abomination of desolation that was going to occur some time after Daniel's prophecy (Dan. 9:27, 11:31, 12:11). The event he described did occur before Christ's birth, between 175–165 BC, when Antiochus IV, the Syrian king, ruled Palestine. During this time, the Syrian king proclaimed himself to be "God." Daniel reported that he gained his throne by "intrigue" and attempted to do away with the Jewish religion all together. Adding insult to injury, he desecrated the temple in Jerusalem by sacrificing a pig (the most ceremonially unclean animal known to Jews) on the altar, and then, he forced the Jewish priests to eat its flesh. He also set up an idol of Zeus in their temple. This "abomination" was meant to demoralize the Jews, and to defile their temple. It was seen as a slap in the face to them and their God.

A similar event occurred following Christ's death in AD 70. At this event, the temple was desecrated and destroyed by Titus and his army, and the Jewish sacrificial system was stopped all together. It was another dark day in the lives of the Jews.

Jesus taught that an abomination that would cause desolation, similar to the one Daniel had foretold, would also occur during the final days (Mt. 24:15–22). This abomination will be significant for at least one very important reason. Paul promised that the timing of the return of Christ would be tied directly to this abomination. This is another major weakness in the pretribulational theory.

Understanding this connection is critically important to establishing a biblical timeline of the second coming. Paul wrote:

> *Concerning the coming of our Lord Jesus Christ and our being gathered to him, we ask you, brothers, not to become easily unsettled or alarmed by some prophecy, report or letter supposed to have come from us, saying that the day of the Lord has already come. Don't let anyone deceive you in any way, for that day will not come until the rebellion occurs and the man of lawlessness is revealed, the man doomed to destruction. He will oppose and will exalt himself over everything that is called God or is worshiped, so that he sets himself up in God's temple, proclaiming himself to be God* (2 Thess. 2:1–4).

Allow me a moment to explain the context surrounding Paul's statement. Paul had invested time with the church of Thessalonica, instructing them concerning the second coming of Christ. Then, after he left, false teachers came into the church and tried to confuse the believers. These false teachers claimed that Paul had written to say the rapture had already occurred and the day of God's wrath had come. That would mean that somehow these believers had missed the rapture. They were understandably upset.

In an attempt to correct the false information and reassure the believers that they had not missed Christ's return, Paul immediately returned their attention to the timeline of events he had previously given them.

He clearly stated:

> *Concerning the coming of our Lord Jesus Christ and our being gathered to him, we ask you, brothers, not to become easily unsettled or alarmed by some prophecy, report or letter supposed to have come from us, saying that the day of the Lord has already come. Don't let anyone deceive you in any way, for that day will not come until the rebellion occurs and the man of lawlessness is revealed* (2 Thess. 2:1–3).

Notice the three events Paul mentioned: the rapture, the day of the Lord, and the rebellion where the man of lawlessness is revealed. The rapture is the gathering up of all believers to be with Christ at His second coming. The day of the Lord is a reference to the day that God's wrath will be poured out on His enemies. Finally, the rebellion, where the man of lawlessness is revealed, is a reference to the event elsewhere described as the Abomination of Desolation.

Take a second to read Paul's words again, this time noting the order he established for them to occur. The rapture will precede the pouring out of God's wrath. However, neither of these events will occur before the Abomination of Desolation (the revealing of the man of lawlessness). This event was required to happen **before** the second coming of Christ could occur. Obviously, from Paul's remarks, the Abomination of Desolation, which was required to occur prior to the return of Christ, had not yet occurred. Therefore, the believers of Paul's day could know that they had not missed the rapture.

Paul's statement does not mean that the rapture and the pouring out of God's wrath have to happen **at** *the exact moment* of the abomination, but they certainly cannot occur **before** that event. Jesus Himself placed that event in the midst of the time of tribulation, which will occur near the end (Mt. 24:15). This confirms that there can be no rapture prior to the time of tribulation. To teach otherwise is to create confusion where God intended to bring clarity. That is exactly what the false teachers of Paul's day were doing, and that is exactly the kind of teachings Paul set out to correct.

It Maintains a Separation, Which Christ Died to Abolish

Another reason the supporters of pretribulationalism insist that the rapture will occur before the tribulation is due to a foundational tenet of dispensationalism, which has been "married" to pretribulationalism. Dispensationalism insists that a clear distinction be maintained between God's dealings with the Church and His dealings with the Jews. This teaching clearly ignores the New Testament teaching that the wall of hostility has been abolished by Christ and that the two groups have been made one in Christ (Eph. 2:13–16). For some reason, unknown to me, they refuse to allow that to happen. So, to maintain this distinction, those who hold to this view claim that the Church will be removed from the earth before God begins dealing with the hearts of the Jews in the final days. Even though they lack biblical evidence for the timing of such an event, they insist upon it in order to make their theory work. In reality, they have allowed their theory to dictate their theology, instead of allowing their theology to dictate their theory. In so doing, they have allowed the tail to wag the dog.

As you can clearly see, there are some major theological problems with the pretribulational view of the rapture. When I discovered these things, I felt I had reached a point of no return. Something had changed within me. I could not go back to what I had previously believed. The search began for what the Bible revealed to be true. Nothing else would satisfy my soul.

CHAPTER TWO

A DANGEROUS DEVIATION

The more I learned about the dispensational theology, which had influenced the pretribulational view of the rapture, the more disturbed I became with what I discovered. I am not alone. Many young theologians who cut their teeth on this type of theology have discovered its flaws and are working hard to reform it, but they are facing an uphill battle. They would like to bring it in line with Scripture without abandoning it all together. While I am thankful for their efforts to reform a theology that is in error, I am still concerned about the widespread acceptance this theory has gained in less than two hundred years. Many unsuspecting people have been led to believe the errors it puts forth.

If there are so many holes in the dispensational pretribulation view of the rapture, we should question how and why it became so popular. When I examined the history of this theory I made some interesting discoveries. First of all, this theory has not been widely embraced for very long. In the early 1800s, a woman named Margaret Macdonald reported seeing a vision which she recorded and shared with others. Her views were later embraced by Edward Irving, John Nelson Darby, and a group called the Plymouth Brethren.

In the 1830s, Darby began teaching his own version of Macdonald's prophecy to which he added the dispensational twist, thus marrying the two theories. He was able to capture the hearts of many in the conservative coalition because he insisted that his teaching was based on a strictly literal interpretation of the Bible. It was not! While some embraced his views, many others regarded his teaching as heretical. However, he was able to convince the Niagara Bible Conference of 1878 that by embracing dispensationalism and its claim of a literal interpretation of the Bible, they could combat the liberalism that was sweeping the land.

C. I. Scofield, a politician and an attorney with a less than flattering track record, liked Darby's theory and was persuaded to include it in a Bible bearing his name: *The Scofield Study Bible.* Scofield's Bible was unlike anything anyone had seen up to that point. It contained footnotes throughout the Bible, offering Scofield's interpretation of the difficult passages. It became the forerunner of the study Bibles we have available today. As Scofield wove Darby's interpretation of the second coming throughout the pages of his Bible, Darby's view began gaining popular acceptance. When unsuspecting people picked up a copy of this Bible and discovered that it offered a detailed explanation of how the events of the end-times would unfold, they soon overlooked the fact that the footnotes lacked the same authority as Scripture. Many simply assumed that if it was written in the Bible it had to be true, disregarding the fact that the footnotes were merely man's opinion. As pastors began to use this Bible, many looked to the footnotes to guide their interpretation, unsuspectingly propagating this false teaching. It was a dangerous deviation from centuries of biblical interpretation.

Through the influence of Scofield's popular study Bible and subsequent materials related to this new theory, dispensationalism began to gain wider acceptance. It was not long before dispensationalism married itself to pretribulationalism, causing the two to appear inseparable. In a very short time, many prominent conservative leaders, desiring a literal interpretation of the Bible, embraced dispensationalism and the pretribulational view it espoused. The tone of their rhetoric seemed to imply that one's refusal to accept the tenets of their new belief system was the equivalent of denying faith in the Bible itself. In other words, if one did not want to be viewed as a liberal, he should wholeheartedly embrace their view. Many did just that.

A great interest in prophetic literature was rekindled when the Jews returned to the land of Israel in 1948 to reestablish the Jewish state. It was not long before movies were being produced depicting what it would be like for those who missed the rapture and had to live through the terrible events associated with the tribulation. These movies helped to reinforce and spread the dispensational view of the rapture.

More recently, this view has been wildly popularized through the fictional book series, *"Left Behind,"* and the subsequent movies that were based upon these books. While this series is correctly classified as fictional, millions of people have lost sight of that fact and have allowed their view of the rapture to be shaped by the content of these stories.

A Word of Caution:

In a very short time—less than two hundred years—a philosophy that was once rejected by serious Bible scholars has been propagated and widely accepted by many unsuspecting people who fill the pews of churches around the world. Shelves in local bookstores are filled with books that also spread this false theory, perhaps because it is so comforting to think that Christians will be allowed to forego all of the suffering that the Bible associates with the final days. To be real honest, this strikes fear in my heart.

However, as my research on this topic progressed, I was amazed to discover how many Bible scholars adamantly reject the dispensational pretribulation view of the rapture due to a lack of biblical support. Their books do not sell as well as their counterparts' books because the truth they contain is much more difficult to swallow.

Christians must guard against building their belief system on a view of the second coming that is not accurate, no matter how popular it may be. What we believe about the second coming is critically important because it will affect how we prepare for the return of Christ. Let's be honest; if we know we will have to endure the difficult days of the end, we will be more likely to prepare ourselves for those days than if we believe we will get to skip the sufferings all together. We don't tend to prepare for things that we think will never occur. No one who lives on top of a mountain buys flood insurance. Those who think they will be exempt from the sufferings of the end will not likely prepare themselves for the hardships they will encounter in those final days. That is a scary thought.

Additionally, those who believe that they can repent and be saved following the rapture will be devastated to discover that they cannot. Jesus clearly warned that His followers are to be ready and waiting when He returns. No further opportunities will be offered after He breaks through the clouds. To teach that salvation will be offered after His return is to set people up for the greatest heartbreak anyone could ever encounter. Many who are misled by this teaching will miss out on eternity with God because they think they will have more time. How tragic! This is one reason a book of this nature is needed in this day.

As you consider what I have to say in the remainder of this book, I simply ask you to remain committed to the truth of God's Word. Again, you should not blindly accept what I am writing any more than you should accept what others have written. Examine what you hold to be true. If your beliefs are true, testing them will only strengthen them. Do your best to set aside what you wish would occur and examine what the Bible records will occur. Reexamine the parables of Jesus in Matthew 25 and note the absence of any second chance for those who are not prepared for His return.

Now, I realize I have unloaded a truck load of information on you in this section. Perhaps it has challenged what you hold to be true. Please don't bail out on me. In the next few sections, things will begin to come together. Keep reading! Your disbelief will soon fade as the Word of God begins to answer many of the questions that are racing through your mind right now. Before long, you may be saying what others have said: "The more I read, the more I understand what God's Word really says." I pray this will be the way you feel by the time you have finished reading this book.

SECTION TWO

BASIC TRAINING

Every good soldier needs to know how to read and interpret a map if they want to end up at the rally point on time. Jesus, understanding how important that date would be for His followers, sat down with His troops, unfolded the map, and explained the terrain that they would be required to traverse before being reunited with Him on that day.

In this next section, we will explore the map Jesus laid out for His disciples concerning the events that would precede their reunion. Jesus answered His disciples' questions concerning when He would return and the signs that would surround that return. Included in His answer is the information we need in order to better understand the rest of the end-time teachings contained in the New Testament.

Jesus sketched the map that the other New Testament writers would later color in. Without the information that Jesus supplied, it would be very difficult to put together a timeline of events leading up to His return. However, if one starts with Jesus' teachings, the other passages in the Bible make much more sense.

Jesus not only listed the critical events that would lead up to His return, but He also urged His followers to get themselves prepared for the opposition they would face during those final days. He warned them to be prepared for the spiritual apathy they would encounter as they lived in a fallen world. He warned of the hostility they would encounter as they took salvation's message to the ends of the earth. As a general preparing his troops for the raging battles that lie ahead, Jesus warned His followers of the conflicts they would one day face.

Jesus also shared three stories with His disciples, illustrating the necessity of being prepared for His return, as well as the danger of living unprepared. These stories were not shared simply to tickle His listener's ears; they were spoken to create a sense of urgency within them to live each day of their lives in eager expectation of His imminent return.

Jesus informed them of the character traits that would distinguish His followers from everyone else in the world. In essence, He handed them the answers to the questions on their final exam ahead of time, and He challenged them to prepare themselves for His return that was sure to come. Knowing the tendency of mankind to postpone preparation until the last possible minute, He warned them of the dangers of doing so.

Jesus used these three parables (earthly stories with heavenly messages) to illustrate three core character traits that would distinguish His true followers from the rest of the world. In each of these parables, the absence of these character traits proved disastrous for those who lacked them.

I cannot emphasize how important the next few chapters will be in the formation of a correct timeline of end-time events. Please don't skip over this section. Follow closely what Jesus has to say and you will save yourself a whole lot of confusion. While I will build most of what I write around Matthew's account, be aware that Mark and Luke also report the same information in their accounts.

CHAPTER THREE
BATTLE PLANS

Have you ever noticed that at every turn Jesus found a way to take the ordinary things of life and turn them into object lessons from which His followers could learn more about Him and His coming kingdom? The particular day we are about to examine in the life of Christ was no different. On this day, as recorded in Matthew 24, His disciples seemed enamored by the magnitude and beauty of the temple in Jerusalem. Unimpressed with the earthly temple, which was a mere shadow of the original one He had no doubt seen in Heaven (Heb. 8:5, 9:24), Jesus warned them not to get too attached to the buildings because they would all come tumbling down one day.

As they sat on the side of the Mount of Olives overlooking Jerusalem, the disciples wanted to clarify His comments concerning the temple's destruction. They asked Him to tell them when this would happen, and what the signs would be leading up to His coming and the end of the age. What they got in response was almost more than they bargained for. Instead of just answering their inquiry, Jesus presented them with a map of the battles that lie ahead.

Matthew recorded Jesus' response to their inquiry in Matthew 24:4–35. It will prove helpful to the rest of our study to get familiar with what Jesus taught concerning the time of His return. In response to the disciples' two-part question, Jesus answered:

> *Watch out that no one deceives you. For many will come in my name, claiming, "I am the Christ," and will deceive many. You will hear of wars and rumors of wars, but see to it that you are not alarmed. Such*

things must happen, but the end is still to come. Nation will rise against nation, and kingdom against kingdom. There will be famines and earthquakes in various places. All these are the beginning of birth pains.

Then you will be handed over to be persecuted and put to death, and you will be hated by all nations because of me. At that time many will turn away from the faith and will betray and hate each other, and many false prophets will appear and deceive many people. Because of the increase of wickedness, the love of most will grow cold, but he who stands firm to the end will be saved. And this gospel of the kingdom will be preached in the whole world as a testimony to all nations, and then the end will come.

So when you see standing in the holy place "the abomination that causes desolation," spoken of through the prophet Daniel—let the reader understand—then let those who are in Judea flee to the mountains. Let no one on the roof of his house go down to take anything out of the house. Let no one in the field go back to get his cloak. How dreadful it will be in those days for pregnant women and nursing mothers! Pray that your flight will not take place in winter or on the Sabbath. For then there will be great distress, unequaled from the beginning of the world until now—and never to be equaled again. If those days had not been cut short, no one would survive, but for the sake of the elect those days will be shortened. At that time if anyone says to you, "Look, here is the Christ!" or, "There he is!" do not believe it. For false Christs and false prophets will appear and perform great signs and miracles to deceive even the elect—if that were possible. See, I have told you ahead of time.

So if anyone tells you, "There he is, out in the desert," do not go out; or, "Here he is, in the inner rooms," do not believe it. For as lightning that comes from the east is visible even in the west, so will be the coming of the Son of Man. Wherever there is a carcass, there the vultures will gather.

Immediately after the distress of those days "the sun will be darkened, and the moon will not give its light; the stars will fall from the sky, and the heavenly bodies will be shaken."

At that time the sign of the Son of Man will appear in the sky, and all the nations of the earth will mourn. They will see the Son of Man coming on the clouds of the sky, with power and great glory. And he will send his angels with a loud trumpet call, and they will gather his elect from the four winds, from one end of the heavens to the other.

Now learn this lesson from the fig tree: As soon as its twigs get tender and its leaves come out, you know that summer is near. Even so, when you see all these things, you know that it is near, right at the door. I tell you the truth, this generation will certainly not pass away until all these things have happened. Heaven and earth will pass away, but my words will never pass away.

Within this passage lies Jesus' map of the events leading up to the end of time. In just a few brief statements, He was able to summarize what His followers would need to know to be successful in the midst of these conflicts. Much like a squadron leader opening up his map of a mountain before his troops and pointing out the enemy strongholds, Jesus unfolded His own map and gave the disciples a glimpse of the mountain that stood before them. As a master teacher, He instructed His followers concerning the events that will precede His second coming.

These instructions were not just for the twelve disciples. They were for all of us who would live between that day and the day of His return. During this time of instruction, Jesus warned His followers of those who would seek to deceive them with false claims and false teachings (Mt. 24:4–5). He hinted of the terrible turmoil that would plague the earth as wars broke out in various places, and as rumors of wars threatened to leave the world devoid of any sense of lasting peace (Mt. 24:6). Even in that type of environment, Jesus said that His followers need not be alarmed because it was all a part of His great plan, which would occur before they were rejoined with Him (Mt. 24:6).

He spoke of nations rising against nations and kingdoms rising against kingdoms (Mt. 24:7). While that sounds repetitious in the English language, in the Greek language, which Jesus spoke, it was not at all repetitious. The word He used for "nations" was the Greek word *ethnos* from which we get our word ethnic. It was a word that was used to describe different races or religions—different people who follow different gods. In a real sense, He was describing racial conflicts and religiously motivated attacks that would occur near the end. The word He used for "kingdom" literally meant "rule" or "realm." While it could simply mean a kingdom as we might imagine it, it could also mean a battle in the spiritual realm. If that were the case, then Jesus was not only warning about the traditional "wars" of verse six, but also of attacks that would be religiously motivated and conflicts that would occur in the spiritual realms.

Another sign indicating that the end is near will be a noticeable increase in the number of natural disasters occurring in various places (Mt. 24:7). These disasters are not limited to one part of the earth, but will occur in many different places. He warned that these types of things were just the beginning of birth pains (Mt. 24:8). In other words, there was more to come, and it would get worse before it got better. Similar to a woman in labor, the pains will start off mild, increase in frequency and intensity, and not cease until the delivery is complete. God will deliver His followers, but until then there will be various trials and tribulations they will be called upon to endure. This, Jesus stated, is all part of His exit strategy.

Jesus warned that Christians would be hated, persecuted, and even put to death because of their faith in Christ (Mt. 24:9). This intense persecution will cause those who are not fully committed to Christ to turn away from Christ and betray those who are genuine in their faith (Mt. 24:10). It will be a sifting of those who merely profess faith in Christ from those who genuinely possess life in Christ. The number of false prophets will increase on the world's stage and the wickedness of the world will greatly increase, causing the love of most to grow cold (Mt. 24:11–12). Only those who possess a saving faith in Christ will be left standing in that day (Mt. 24:13).

While the world is in the midst of great chaos, and the Church is in the midst of great persecution, the gospel of the kingdom of God will be shared with the inhabitants of the whole world. Then, the end will come (Mt. 24:14). With those words, Jesus provided His followers with a general summary of the way things would be prior to His return.

Now, this is very important to grasp. At this point in His conversation with the disciples, Jesus suspended His summary of events and began providing them with a few examples of specific events that would alert them to the fact that those days had arrived. He signaled this transition when he said, "So, when you see . . ." (Mt. 24:15) and, "So, if anyone tells you . . ." (Mt. 24:26). In essence He was saying to them, "Here is an overview of the end, so when you see these specific things you will know that the end is drawing near."

One of the specifics Jesus promised would occur was a terrible abomination, which the prophet Daniel had foretold. This event would unleash a great persecution on the followers of Christ *"unequaled from the beginning of the world until now—and never to be equaled again"* (Mt. 24:21). Jesus warned, *"If those days had not been cut short, no one would survive, but for the sake of the elect those days will be shortened"* (Mt. 24:22). This event would most likely coincide with the time of persecution and death He had mentioned earlier in His instructions (see Mt. 24:9–10).

Jesus also warned that false Christs and false prophets would appear at that time performing great signs and miracles to deceive even the elect—if that were possible (Mt. 24:24). This is a further illustration of what He had just told them in verse eleven. The spirit of deception will be so strong in that day that the followers of Christ will not be able to trust the words of man, but only the Word of God.

Following the great distress He had just described, Jesus warned that there would be one final indicator that His second coming is right around the corner. He promised:

> *Immediately after the distress of those days, "the sun will be darkened, and the moon will not give its light; the stars will fall from the sky, and the heavenly bodies will be shaken." At that time, the sign of the Son of Man will appear in the sky, and all the nations of the earth will mourn. They will see the Son of Man coming on the clouds of the sky, with power and great glory. And he will send his angels with a loud trumpet call, and they will gather his elect from the four winds, from one end of the heavens to the other* (Mt. 24:29–31).

With those words, Jesus completed the unfolding of His exit strategy. At this particular point in time, He did not discuss what would be done with those who refused to follow Him, but He assured His followers that He would take care of them.

The disciples must have been blown away by what they heard on that day. They were already having a difficult time understanding His teachings about the cross of Calvary, much less understanding all that He was sharing about the events surrounding His second coming. The events He was describing must have seemed surreal and overwhelming to them.

Understanding their apprehensiveness, Jesus assured them that He had a plan to see them all the way through to the end. Like a brilliant general on a battlefield, He not only understood the battle that lay ahead, but He developed a plan to get them all to the rally point where He would rejoin them. By sharing this information with His disciples on that day, He was laying out His battle plans before leading His troops onto the battlefield. It was a bold move designed to bring a confident assurance to each of His followers that He was in control, despite what their eyes might see and their hearts might feel. Some two thousand years later, those words still offer us the confident assurance that He is in control and His plan is still in effect.

As we seek to understand the finer details of Jesus' response, it is helpful to note that the disciples asked Him two questions on that day, not just one. First, they asked when the destruction of the temple would occur. Next, they asked what signs they should look for leading up to His coming and the end of the age. In order to correctly interpret Jesus' response, one must first determine if He answered both of their questions, or only one of them. If He only answered one of their questions, which question did His response address? This may sound like a nit-picky inquiry, but it is critical when seeking to establish a correct timeline.

Some believe that Jesus' response addressed both of the questions that the disciples asked. Most likely, this is what the disciples would have understood. In their minds, they probably could not imagine anything worse than the overthrow of their nation and the destruction of their temple. They probably assumed that if those things were to ever happen, the end of all things was near. In other words, in their minds they may have had a difficult time separating the destruction of their temple and the end of the world.

When one compares the historical evidence of the temple's destruction in AD 70 at the hands of Titus and his army, that event appears very similar to Jesus' comment about the abomination that would cause desolation (Mt. 24:4–20). Total devastation resulted from the Titus invasion. The only people who survived were those who ran for their lives. When Titus' army was finished overthrowing Jerusalem, the Jewish temple was destroyed and left completely desolate. What he and his army did was an incredible abomination in the eyes of the Jews.

Since Jesus' prediction seems very similar to those actual events, some insist that Jesus was warning the disciples of the temple's destruction at the hands of Titus. Had Jesus' comments stopped with His description of the great abomination in verse twenty, there would be little doubt that He was referring to that event. However, His response did not stop there. While certain parts of Jesus' description fit that event perfectly, there were other parts of Jesus' prediction that did not fit the devastation that occurred at the hands of Titus and his army.

For example, Jesus promised that certain things would occur at that time, which did not occur in AD 70. He stated that there would be *"great distress, unequaled from the beginning of the world until now—and never to be equaled again. If those days had not been cut short, no one would survive, but for the sake of the elect those days will be shortened"* (Mt. 24:21–22). While the destruction was heartbreaking and devastating to the Jews, the damage and destruction was localized. It only affected the Jewish nation, not the world as a whole. It is hard to imagine that those events would have been worse than the flood

(Gen. 6–8), or worse than the time of tribulation mentioned throughout the book of Revelation. In fact, both, the events of Noah's day and the events described in Revelation, seem to easily trump the events of AD 70. Furthermore, there is no evidence that the days during the temple's destruction were "cut short" in an effort to spare the lives of God's people.

Jesus made another prediction that was not fulfilled during the time of the temple's destruction. He said, *"Immediately after the distress of those days"* the sun would be darkened and the moon would not give its light. He claimed that the stars would fall from the sky, and the heavens would be shaken. He also promised that His return for His followers would occur in conjunction with the events He had listed. These events did not happen in that day. Opponents of this theory insist that for these reasons, one cannot limit Jesus' response to the event in AD 70. Their critique is a fair one.

If His comments cannot be limited to the destruction of Jerusalem in AD 70, was Jesus answering both questions in one statement? Was the first part of His response addressing the destruction of Jerusalem and the second half of His response addressing His second coming? If that were the case, then it would seem that His second coming would have followed closely on the heels of the temple's destruction. It obviously did not! So, for that reason, His comments cannot be understood as addressing both questions directly.

That seems to leave us with only one other option. It would seem that Jesus must have neglected to directly answer their first question concerning the destruction of the temple, and instead, answered only the second question concerning the events leading up to His second coming. However, if one seeks to apply Jesus' response to the second coming question, another problem seems to arise. Jesus stated toward the end of His response, *"This generation will certainly not pass away until all these things have happened"* (Mt. 24:34). Some argue that He could not have been speaking of the second coming because all of the events He mentioned, including His second coming, did not occur before the disciples' generation passed away! Their objection must be carefully considered.

Since it is understood by Christians that Jesus never stated something that was not true, somehow these two issues must be reconciled.

Is it possible for Jesus' statements to be applied to the events leading up to His second coming without contradicting His statement about the generation not passing away before all these things occur? Yes, it is possible! In fact, everything that Jesus predicted in His response is described elsewhere in Scripture as occurring in the last days. The only part of Jesus' response that seems to hinder this interpretation is the promise that "this generation" would not pass away until all these things happened. That problem can be easily resolved when one carefully examines the context of Jesus' statement. It is not as difficult as it might seem.

Once again, understanding the context of Jesus' remarks is essential to a correct interpretation. When Jesus made the statement we are currently considering, He had concluded His description of the events that would occur before His return, and He had introduced a fig tree as an object lesson to describe how the disciples might recognize that His return was right around the corner. He taught that just as a fig tender could look at the twigs and leaves on a fig tree and determine that summer was near, so the generation that was alive just prior to His return would be able to look at the events He had just described and know that the end was drawing near (Mt. 24:32–33). It was in that context that He stated, *"This generation will certainly not pass away until all these things have happened"* (Mt. 24:34). Although the disciples might have assumed that His statement was referring to their own generation, it obviously did not because Jesus did not return before their generation passed away. The dilemma is solved as one understands that Jesus was referring to the generation that will be alive when the events He had just listed began to unfold. In fact, this is the only explanation that makes sense. "This generation" refers to the final generation before Jesus' return—the generation that is alive to witness the events that Jesus had just described, not the disciples' generation.

Jesus was not telling the disciples that they would be around when He returned; He was stating that the generation that witnessed the beginning of these events would still be around when the events reached their conclusion. In other words, these terrifying events would not drag on over a long period of time. The events surrounding His second coming would all occur within the span of one generation. Once the events He had mentioned began to unfold, they would unfold quite rapidly. This interpretation corresponds with Jesus' comparison of these events to the labor pains of a pregnant woman (Mt. 24:8). The "labor pains" would seem mild at first, then they would increase in both frequency and intensity, but they would not last for long. John's time table in the book of Revelation reveals the same to be true.

Some try to insist that we interpret the passage in the same way the disciples understood it, but that argument does not hold weight. Many, if not most, of the teachings Jesus presented to the disciples concerning His death, resurrection, and return were misinterpreted by the disciples. Stop for just a minute and reflect upon how many times He had to reinstruct them concerning the cross? It was only after the cross, His resurrection, and the indwelling of the Holy Spirit, that the disciples finally began to grasp what He really meant. This statement is no different.

Therefore, Jesus' response to the disciples' question should be understood as applying to the events just prior to His second coming. The amazing thing about the way Jesus answered their question is that His answer also provided them with the instruction they needed to be able to live through the difficult days that they would face in their own lifetime, including the difficult days during the destruction of the temple in AD 70. So, while Jesus addressed the second question directly, He also dealt with their first question indirectly.

In fact, Jesus answered the disciples' question in such a way as to challenge each generation since that day to prepare for the adversities that each generation would face. His response challenges each generation to face its own set of adversities with an eye on eternity. As believers, we do not need to know the exact time of certain events in our day, or the exact time of His return. We simply need to live each day as the disciples did, with the hopeful expectation that He could return within our lifetime. While it is important for us to recognize the events that will signal the beginning of the end, it is more important for us to know how to prepare ourselves for the day we meet Christ face to face. It is our responsibility to be found faithfully following Christ on that day.

CHAPTER FOUR

PREVAILING WINDS

Determining the correct order of the events of the end-times is not enough! As wonderful as that might seem, it is of little value unless that knowledge is translated into action. It must be allowed to transform the priorities of our lives. It must alter why we live and who we live for. Knowledge of this type must become transformational—life changing! It must be woven into the very fabric of our lives. In short, it must become the blueprint of our lives.

Christ, an all-knowing member of the Holy Trinity, knows every battle that believers will ever face. He not only knows the battles, but He has developed an incredible battle plan complete with an exit strategy and victory party that will follow. Before He returned to His Father, He shared with His followers what they should expect as the time draws near for His return.

Jesus told His disciples that upon His return all the nations of the earth would mourn (Mt. 24:30). Have you ever wondered why the nations of the earth would mourn at such an incredible event? It is because that day will be a bittersweet day. It will be sweet for those who have prepared themselves by following Christ, but bitter for those who have not. People all around the world will mourn on that day because many will discover they failed to make the proper preparations for His return, and on that day it will be too late.

The disciples must have been anxious to know the exact timing of His plan. Can't you hear the wheels turning in their heads? They must have been thinking to themselves, "Cut to the chase, Jesus, and just tell us the day and the hour." Almost faster than they could think it, Jesus burst their bubble by saying, *"No one knows about that day or hour, not even the angels in heaven, nor the Son, but only the Father"* (Mt. 24:36). Evidently, it was not important that they know the exact day or hour. What was important was for them to prepare themselves for the trying times ahead.

Wanting to further prepare His followers for what they could expect in those final days, Jesus described the spiritual condition of the world at the time of His return. He said, *"As it was in the days of Noah, so it will be at the coming of the Son of Man. For in the days before the flood, people were eating and drinking, marrying and giving in marriage, up to the day Noah entered the ark, and they knew nothing about what would happen until the flood came and took them all away. That is how it will be at the coming of the Son of Man"* (Mt. 24:37–39).

I know you must be familiar with the story of Noah. Think about the spiritual condition of the world right before the flood. Genesis 6:5–6 tells us, *"The LORD saw how great man's wickedness on the earth had become, and that every inclination of the thoughts of his heart was only evil all the time. The LORD was grieved that he had made man on the earth, and his heart was filled with pain."* A mere six chapters into the biblical record we are told that the spiritual climate in Noah's day had reached an all-time low. The people of that day had cast off all restraints. They did as they pleased, and they were so consumed with earthly things they had no thought for the eternal. They simply lived for the moment. Pleasure was the god at whose altar they worshiped. Notice what occupied the center of their lives—self, not God. Their hearts had turned far from God and had become *"only evil all the time."*

Jesus taught that the spiritual climate of the world immediately preceding His return would be very similar to the spiritual climate of the world just prior to the flood. His followers would need to prepare themselves to stand in those difficult days, even if it meant that they had to stand alone.

He also pointed to another similarity between Noah's day and the day of His return. In Noah's day, the people of the world were caught completely by surprise when the rain began to fall and the rivers began to rise. It was not because they had not been warned by Noah time and time again. He had not kept the pending judgment of God a secret. He warned his world of the coming judgment day after day, even to the point that God gave him the title, *"Preacher of righteousness"* (2 Pet. 2:5). The people of his day were caught by surprise because they refused to heed the warnings Noah had issued. It was easier to laugh at Noah and the boat in his yard than for them to admit their wickedness and repent. Besides, rain seemed highly unlikely since they had never seen it before. Thus, they dismissed Noah as another preacher with an axe to grind, and instead of preparing themselves for the impending doom that lay on the horizon, they poked fun at God's messenger while reveling in their sinfulness. They ignored the warnings until it was too late. The door of the ark was shut, the rain began to fall, and at that moment, nobody was found laughing.

Any talk about the events of the end-times will seem as strange to the people living in the final days as rain sounded to the people of Noah's day. It will prove easier and more comfortable for them to poke fun at the messenger and the message, than to heed the warnings, repent, and make preparations. Perhaps that is why Jesus described the road that leads to life as narrow and less traveled, while the road to destruction is described as wide and filled with travelers headed to a terrible, unimaginable eternity (Mt. 7:13–14).

Another similarity worth noting between Noah's day and the last days is the terrible judgment and destruction that awaited all who ignored the warnings. In Noah's day, the only ones willing to listen to the warnings were the members of Noah's own family. How difficult it must have been for him to remain faithful to God while the rest of the world laughed and went their own way. Many today laugh when they are urged to prepare for Christ's return, but no one will be laughing when they miss out on eternity with God. Understanding the everlasting destruction that awaits the unrepentant, Jesus urged all who would listen to Him to make personal preparation for His return, and to warn others to do the same.

When someone is told that tough times lie ahead, it is understandable for him or her to feel a certain level of apprehension. Many believers seem terrified of facing the events of the end, but they should recall one other thing about Noah's day. While God was destroying all that was wicked on the earth, He was carefully protecting and providing for Noah and his family. The very water that wrought destruction on the world's wicked population also served to carry Noah and his family to safety. We need not fear because

God is able to offer the same type of deliverance to His followers in the final days. He will see us through to the end.

Jesus informed the disciples that on the day of His return men and women will be carrying on business as usual. They will get up and head off to work as they always have. They will go through the motions of their daily routine with little thought for what is on the horizon. Then suddenly, without any delay, Christ will appear, and their fate will be sealed. Jesus illustrated this fact with a story about two people who will be working together on that day. One will be taken away while the other will be left behind (Mt. 24:40–41). It will seem like any other day to them until Christ breaks through the clouds to gather those who belong to Him.

So, what are Christians to do in the meantime? How are they to prepare? In the remainder of Matthew 24, Jesus focused on two things His followers need to do in order to be prepared for His return. First, He warned that they should *"keep watch . . . and be ready"* (Mt. 24:42–44). In other words, they should live life on high alert, not ignoring the signs of the times. They should live with their eyes opened wide to His activity and with their hearts sensitive to His voice. They should know how to interpret the events of that day and make preparations accordingly.

The events of September 11, 2001 taught Americans the value of being prepared ahead of time. Most of us in America never imagined that our country was vulnerable to attack, but we were sadly mistaken. The attack did not look like anything we had ever even imagined. Thinking that we were safe, we did little to prepare for that type of attack. Looking back on that event, we would all agree that it is better to be ready and be wrong, than to be wrong and not be ready. The same is true concerning our preparation for Christ's return.

Many Christians of previous generations believed they were living in the last days, only to die before Christ returned. I promise you they have no regrets. The fact that Christ did not come in their day is no reason for Christians to live with no expectancy today. Better to live life prepared for Christ's imminent return and die as a faithful follower of Christ, than to have Christ return and be found unprepared.

Secondly, Christians should be faithfully following after Christ. In other words, He expects to find His followers doing the things He has purposed for them to do. As faithful followers, they are to set aside their own agenda and live for Him. This level of faithfulness is a mark that is to distinguish His true followers from the rest of the world.

The one who calls himself a disciple of Christ, but lives only for himself, taking lightly the call to faithfulness, will be surprised when Christ returns and assigns him a place with the hypocrites in Hell (Mt. 24:48–51). In fact, Jesus warned that not everyone who claims to be His follower is a true follower, but rather, only those who *"do the will of the Father in heaven"* (Mt. 7:21). His followers are to be busy doing the work of the Father. Thus, Christ warned them to make sure they are *"found faithful"* upon His return (Mt. 24:45–51).

During the final days, many people will develop calloused hearts and scoff at the idea that Christ is coming again soon (2 Pet. 3:3–15). They will point to the fact that every generation before them has thought that they were the generation that would see Christ's return, yet He has not appeared. Because they think they have plenty of time, they will fail to prepare themselves. Thinking His return is still far off, they will gladly embark upon their own agenda instead of God's agenda. By doing this, their ways will become evil in the eyes of the Lord.

Christians, however, are not to live as the rest of the world lives. They are called to live with their hope set fully on Christ. As children of God, they are called to be faithful stewards of God's grace in its various forms. They are to use their time, talents, gifts, resources, influence, and everything else God gives to them for the furtherance of His kingdom. Jesus reminded His followers that rewards await those who are faithful, and judgment awaits those who are not.

I remind you, it is not enough to know the details of His second coming. That knowledge must transform who we are, why we live, and who we live for!

CHAPTER FIVE
READY OR NOT!

Great leaders, military or otherwise, set their followers up for success. They do so by preparing them for the events they will encounter so that they are not caught unprepared. Jesus did exactly the same thing by sharing stories with His followers that conveyed truths and information they needed to know to succeed. These next few chapters will examine a few of those stories related to His second coming.

Sticking with the theme of preparedness, Jesus shared with His disciples a parable that related to His second coming. It was a story about ten Jewish bridesmaids. Matthew called them "virgins." Jesus' disciples, immersed in that culture, would have immediately understood the background of the story Jesus was telling them. However, since the wedding customs of our day are far different than theirs, a little background information will prove helpful for us at this point.

According to many experts, a marriage ceremony was the single greatest celebration and social event in Jewish culture. The lengthy process leading up to most Jewish weddings involved three stages: the engagement, the betrothal, and the presentation of the couple at the wedding feast. The engagement period began long before the boy and girl reached the marrying age of thirteen or fourteen. Since the children were too young to make such an important decision, the arrangement of the marriage was usually worked out by their fathers. The groom's father typically offered the bride's father a gift commonly known as "the bride price" in exchange for the promise of his daughter's hand in marriage. If the offer was acceptable, the deal would be sealed by the paying of a deposit guaranteeing full payment would be made at the marriage ceremony. At this point in the process, the engagement would be considered the equivalent of a marriage contract.

The second stage of the process was the betrothal period, which began with a ceremony where the couple would exchange their vows, make their commitments to each other, and formally be recognized as pledged to one another. These betrothal vows were legally binding and could be broken only by a formal divorce. You will remember that this was the stage at which Joseph and Mary found themselves when it became known that she was pregnant with Jesus. After the betrothal ceremony, the boy and the girl would each return to their own parent's home to prepare for the final stage, which began with the big day of presentation.

The son, along with the help of his father, would begin preparing a place for the newlyweds to live. This usually involved adding a suite onto his father's house into which they would move after the wedding ceremony. The betrothal period could last many months. If the groom were to die before the presentation ceremony, the woman would be considered a widow even though they had never consummated their marriage or lived together. When the groom had finished all his preparations, the father would send him to get his bride and bring her to the presentation celebration.

While the son was preparing a place for the couple to live, the bride was to be busy preparing herself for the big day when her groom would return for her. She was expected to remain pure and faithful to her betrothed spouse. She was to select her bridesmaids and have them with her on the day of presentation. As they received word that the time was drawing near for the groom to return, the bride and bridesmaids would gather at the bride's home and wait for his arrival. They were expected to be ready at a moment's notice.

One of the items the bridesmaids were expected to have with them was a torch that they could quickly soak in an oil jar, light, and use to lead the way to the celebration. The torch served as more than just an instrument to light the path. It also served as a symbol that identified the members of the wedding party.

When the time came for the presentation celebration to begin, the groom and his groomsmen would head to the bride's home to gather the bridal party for the big feast. It was common for the groom to come during the evening hours with a loud shout of celebration alerting all of his friends and neighbors that the celebration was about to begin. When the bride and her bridesmaids heard his voice, they would run out to meet him with their torches lit.

This feast could last up to a week depending upon the wealth of the families involved. Toward the end of the feast the best man would take the hand of the bride and place it in the hand of the groom, and the couple would head off to the bridal chamber where they would be alone for the very first time. The marriage would be consummated, and the couple would live together as husband and wife from that day forward.

This Jewish custom served as an object lesson that Christ used to teach His followers about the importance of being prepared for His return. Since this custom was common in their day, Jesus' word picture would have been etched in their memory.

In fact, this was not the only time Jesus used this imagery to teach His disciples of His second coming. In John 14, Jesus compared His death, departure, and second coming to that of a Jewish groom who would leave his bride in order to go and prepare a place for the two of them to live. Then, he would return to take her to be with him forever. He said to them:

> *"Do not let your hearts be troubled. Trust in God; trust also in me. In my Father's house are many rooms; if it were not so, I would have told you. I am going there to prepare a place for you. And if I go and prepare a place for you, I will come back and take you to be with me that you also may be where I am . . . I am the way and the truth and the life. No one comes to the Father except through me"* (Jn. 14:1–3, 6).

Think for just a minute about all God has done to make that day possible for us. He made all the arrangements for us to be able to spend eternity with His Son long before we were able to comprehend His love for us. He paid the bride's price with His Son's blood shed on the cross of Calvary. He gave the Holy Spirit as a deposit guaranteeing all that was yet to come. He matured us to the point that we could express our dependence and devotion to His Son, enabling us to be declared His legal bride. Then, He called Christ home to Heaven to prepare a place for us to spend eternity with Him. Soon, Christ will return to take us to be with Him forever. What a great celebration that will be as our relationship with Him is finally made complete in Heaven. Until that day, we are to be watching, waiting, and faithfully preparing ourselves for His return. Wow! What an incredible picture of all that God has done to enable us to become the Bride of Christ!

Jesus used the story of the ten bridesmaids to tie all of these elements together and to warn His followers of the importance of being prepared for His imminent return. As with the other parables that Jesus taught, this parable had a central message that He wanted to convey (see Mt. 25:1–13).

Now, back to our story! Ten bridesmaids were gathered together, no doubt excited about the groom's imminent return. Remember, these celebrations were a huge deal in that day. We are told that all ten had their lamps (literally torches) and were waiting anxiously for the groom to arrive and the celebration to begin.

Suddenly, without warning, Jesus divided the ten girls into two groups. Five were declared wise, and five were labeled fools. What distinguished one group from the other? Jesus wasted little time in revealing the answer: five brought jars filled with oil, and five did not. That may not seem like a big deal to you, but it was a huge deal in that day. Remember, a lit torch was required in order for the members of the wedding party to go out and meet the groom.

The foolish girls not only forgot to bring any oil to the bride's home, they also failed to recognize their problem until it was too late. Had they recognized their shortcoming before the shops in town had closed, they could have gone to town and purchased some oil while they anticipated the groom's arrival. They had no one to blame but themselves. They had been given plenty of time to get prepared. In fact, Jesus said the groom had delayed his return so long that they had grown sleepy and even taken a nap. They probably thought to themselves, *I've got time to take care of that tomorrow!* That decision is what earned them the title "foolish."

At midnight, when the cry rang out, signifying the groom's arrival, the five foolish bridesmaids immediately knew they were in trouble. After unsuccessfully trying to borrow some oil from those who were prepared for that moment, they left in search of some oil of their own. It is doubtful that any oil shops were opened at that time of the night. Either way, while they were gone, trying to do what they should have already done, the bridegroom arrived! The five who were prepared were ushered into the banquet hall, and the Bible says, *"The door was shut"* (Mt. 25:10).

Some time later, the five foolish bridesmaids showed up at the celebration and begged to be let in, but the bridegroom refused. The decision of the five foolish bridesmaids to postpone their preparation caused them to miss the arrival of the groom and the celebration that followed. Their opportunity to be a part of the celebration had been missed. No second chance was offered to them!

Making sure the disciples did not miss the whole point of His story Jesus sets the hook, as a fisherman would set the hook on a fish that was nibbling on his bait. Jesus says, *"Therefore . . ."* (for this very reason), *"keep watch, because you do not know the day or the hour"* (Mt. 25:13). I believe Jesus was warning them to double check to make sure they were ready for His return. He was also illustrating that there will be no second chances for those who postpone their preparations. One's preparation must be made ahead of time, not after the fact.

In a day when our world has been lulled to sleep by teachers who insist there will be a "second chance" for those who are "left behind" at Christ's return, we need to hear and heed the message of Christ. Now is the time to get prepared. Now is the time for men and women to repent and come into a personal relationship with Jesus Christ.

I am fearful that churches around the world are filled with men and women who are similar to the five foolish bridesmaids. They are all dressed up with nowhere to go. They gather at the bride's house (church). They clothe themselves with garments of good works. They carry a torch that has yet to be lit. They sing and talk about the celebration that is to come, yet they lack the oil they need for the journey that is ahead. Most of them know down deep inside that they are lacking something, but they have convinced themselves they still have time, or they will somehow be offered a second chance. Maybe tomorrow, they foolishly tell themselves, but tomorrow never seems to arrive.

The five foolish bridesmaids lacked oil for their lamps. It is the absence of this oil that distinguished them from the wise bridesmaids. What did the oil symbolize? I believe it represents the presence of the Holy Spirit that abides in all who genuinely belong to Christ (Rom. 8:9). Those who lack the presence of the Holy Spirit lack the relationship with Jesus that is required in order to be admitted into the heavenly celebration (1 Jn. 5:12). Jesus made it clear that a relationship with Him is the only ticket into Heaven (Jn. 14:6). Those who lack that personal relationship with Jesus will face the same fate as the foolish bridesmaids who were told by the groom, *"I tell you the truth, I don't know you"* (Mt. 25:12). At that time it will be too late. No second chances will be offered to make things right.

Jesus is returning soon, and He made it crystal clear that now is the time for those who want to attend the celebration to get themselves prepared.

CHAPTER SIX

FRIEND OR FOE?

The Bible makes it abundantly clear that our actions reveal the true nature of our hearts. In other words, what is on the inside always works its way out. While we can pretend to be something we are not, eventually the truth will surface, exposing the very things we have worked hard to keep hidden. When a person's heart has been changed by God through spiritual rebirth, that heart will always seek tangible ways to express to God the never-ending gratitude that forever flows from within it. A genuine salvation experience forever changes who a person is and what that person values most. A heart that belongs to God seeks ways to invest itself in the things that are foremost on the heart of God.

In Matthew 25:14–30, Jesus shared with His disciples another parable concerning His second coming. This time, He focused on the type of heart He will be looking for upon His return. He made it abundantly clear that the hearts of His followers would be different from the hearts of others who were simply going through the motions—still lacking a genuine relationship with Him.

In this parable, Jesus warns us not to be fooled by the many people who attend church weekly, giving the outward impression that they have been inwardly transformed while their hearts still lack a lifesaving, life-changing relationship with God. They profess to have something they do not yet possess—the life-giving presence of the Holy Spirit. They may be a part of a local congregation, but they are not part of the eternal family of God. They may pretend to be a friend of God when in reality they are His foe.

Jesus illustrated this truth through a story about three servants who were given the opportunity to manage a portion of their master's resources while he was gone on a trip. The way each one handled the resources entrusted to him revealed the type of heart each man possessed. In this story, all three servants were entrusted with different portions of their master's estate to manage for him. The size of the "portfolio" was based upon what the master knew each servant would be able to handle. They were expected to manage what he had given them until he returned, at which time each servant would be called in to give a full account of what each had accomplished.

The servant who was given the largest portfolio immediately went to work investing what he had been given. He worked until the day the master returned, and was able to double the investment of his master. When the master returned and performed his audit, the servant reported the earnings that he had produced for the master's estate. The master's response was very favorable: *"Well done, good and faithful servant! You have been faithful with a few things I will put you in charge of many things. Come and share your master's happiness"* (Mt. 25:21).

Just like the first servant, the second servant also went to work immediately. He too worked until the day the master returned, and he was able to double his master's investment. Although his return on investment was not as large as the first servant's earnings, it represented the same degree of faithfulness on his part. When he appeared before the master to give his full report, he received the same favorable commendation from the master as the first servant.

The third servant's fate was quite different. When he received his lot from the master, he immediately dug a hole and buried it in the ground. He did not attempt to use what the master had given him in order to gain an increase for the master's estate. He did what many people do with the things they have been given by God . . . nothing!

When the master returned and began his audit, the servant immediately began to make excuses. He looked for others to blame for his poor stewardship. He even tried to call into question the character of the master whom he had pledged to serve. He accused the master of being a hard man to serve, a man who took what was not his, and a man whose fearful tactics left his servants unable to do anything productive. The master was not fooled, nor was he impressed! His response was straight to the point: *"You wicked, lazy servant!"* (Mt. 25:26). He exposed the falsehoods imbedded in the servant's charges against him by revealing that if the servant really believed what he had just said about the master, he would have invested the portfolio at the local bank and gained simple interest in order to avoid the master's wrath.

Instead of receiving a commendation from the master, an order was issued by the master for all that had been entrusted to the servant to be taken away and given to one who was willing to use it for the master's benefit. Then, the worthless servant was removed from the master's property. He was banned from the master's presence because the wickedness of his heart had been exposed by his own actions. He was not a true servant. He was a disloyal, unloving pretender. He was little more than a freeloader, willing to take from the master, but unwilling to work for the master. The true motives of his heart had been exposed for all to see.

Each of the three servants shared many things in common. All three enjoyed the generosity of their master. All three servants would have enjoyed free food, proper clothing, and adequate housing—all generously supplied by the master. This particular master even allowed each of his servants to become personal stewards of a portion of his great estate. All three had the same opportunity to prove their faithfulness to the master. However, only two proved to be faithful to the master, while the third one proved to be wicked, lazy, and worthless. For all three, their actions had revealed the true condition of their heart.

Through this story Jesus taught several important lessons. First, God takes the stewardship of His resources very seriously. God has entrusted each person with certain talents, which are to be used for His purposes. Our time, our talents, our gifts, our abilities, our influence, our finances, our passions—all of these make up the portfolio of which God has called us to be careful stewards. As servants/stewards, these resources do not belong to us. We are not the owners, but simply the stewards—the managers of the portfolio. There will be a day when each person will be called to give an account to God of what they have done with the things God has entrusted to their care. The size of the portfolio that God has entrusted to each one is not of primary concern. God decides what He will entrust to our care, and we determine what we do with those gifts. All the friends will be rewarded by their gracious master, while all the foes will be exposed and expelled.

Second, Jesus reminds us that the condition of our hearts will be revealed by what we do with what God has entrusted to us. Those who are true servants of God will prove the genuineness of their relationship by the way they handle the things God places in their care. In the same way, those who are freeloading pretenders will also have their hearts exposed by their actions. What is hidden deep below the surface, in the recesses of the heart, will ultimately be revealed for all to see, be it good or bad.

What we choose to do with the gifts God has given to us is a direct reflection of the condition of our hearts. A regenerate heart that has been changed by the indwelling presence of the Holy Spirit will work for the glory of God until the day Christ returns. The unregenerate heart will demonstrate little concern for the things of God. While a true servant is primarily concerned with living a life pleasing to God, the pretender is preoccupied with little more than his own agenda. He lives for the moment with little thought for eternity, and when called to give an account of his actions, he will unsuccessfully search for a way to shift the blame to someone else.

We must understand that if a person professes to be a servant but never gets around to serving, he is not really a servant. Many people profess to be one thing while their actions scream something totally to the contrary. They may claim to be a Christian without ever serving the cause of Christ. I ask you, are they genuine servants of Christ, or simply pretenders who will one day be exposed? They appear to be something that they are not. Jesus lets it be known that the truth will one day surface.

Third, Jesus warns that the condition of a person's heart, as revealed through their actions, will determine their eternal destiny. It is important to remember that this story was told in the context of a discussion concerning Christ's return and the eternity that is to follow. In this parable, the master represents Christ. The servants who have been entrusted with differing levels of talents represent each of us. When Christ returns and gathers us before Him, each of us will be required to give an account to Him of all that we have done with what He has entrusted to us. It is imperative to understand that our eternal destiny will be determined by the condition of our hearts at His return. The condition of our hearts will be revealed by what we did with what God entrusted to our stewardship. If we genuinely belong to Christ, our actions will consistently demonstrate that fact. If we are not part of His family, our actions will also reveal that truth. Through this story, Jesus is making this point abundantly clear. Salvation is not the result of our works, but genuine salvation always results in good works.

The two servants whose hearts were devoted to their master proved it through their actions, and both were rewarded with access to their master. Their work on the master's behalf paid huge dividends as they were invited to enjoy the fruit of their labor for eternity. However, the servant who was not devoted to the master had the shameful motives of his heart exposed when the master labeled him a wicked, lazy, and worthless servant. His unregenerate heart, and the actions that flowed from it, caused him to be eternally expelled from the master's presence and cast into the darkness where there would be weeping and gnashing of teeth—a phrase that is used throughout the Bible in reference to Hell.

Finally, Jesus' parable demonstrates that once He returns, no other opportunity will be given to make things right with God.

CHAPTER SEVEN

THE GREAT DIVIDE

Following these first two parables, Jesus uses a third story to further illustrate the differences between those who belong to Him and those who do not. This time, He uses the image of a shepherd who is preparing to bed down his animals for the night. Jesus' audience would have been able to relate to this image very easily.

In that day, it was common for sheep and goats to graze together during the day, but at the end of the day, as their shepherd was bedding them down for the night, he would separate the two types of animals. In this particular story, Jesus taught that the sheep would be placed on the right side of the shepherd and the goats would be placed on the shepherd's left side. The sheep are symbolic of the followers of Christ, and the goats are symbolic of everyone else.

In that culture, a person's right side was viewed as a place of great honor and glory. The Bible is replete with many examples of this. For example, when a father was near death, he would send for his oldest son and have him stand on his right side where the father would place his right hand on the son's head and pronounce a blessing upon the child. The Bible also speaks of Christ being exalted to the place of highest honor where He is seated at the right hand of the Father in Heaven.

So, the "sheep" will be placed on the right side of the Shepherd where they will be bestowed great blessings and honor. The "goats" will be placed on the left side of the Shepherd where they will be cursed and exiled to an eternity in Hell.

Jesus painted a stark contrast between the two groups. As a master storyteller, He wanted to draw a clear distinction between the two groups.

He made it clear that there would be no blurring of the lines on that great day. Every person would be placed on one side or the other. There would be no middle ground. Notice He does not say He is going to separate the Baptist from the Catholic or the Methodist from the Episcopalian. He is not going to do this based on one's denomination. He will make the distinction based upon who belongs to Him and who does not.

A very clear distinction is made between the fates of the two groups. To the sheep on His right the Shepherd will say, *"Come, you who are blessed by my Father; take your inheritance, the kingdom prepared for you since the creation of the world"* (Mt. 25:34). To the rest on His left, the Shepherd will say, *"Depart from me, you who are cursed, into the eternal fire prepared for the devil and his angels"* (Mt. 25:41). Notice the distinct differences. One will be told to "come," while the other will be commanded to "depart." One will be called "blessed," while the other will be called "cursed." One will be invited to *"inherit the kingdom prepared for him since the creation of the world,"* while the other will be condemned to *"eternal fire prepared for Satan and his angels."* In verse 46, Jesus explained that the decision He will hand down on that day will have eternal implications. He said those who do not belong to Him will go away to "eternal punishment," while those belonging to Him will enter into "eternal life."

Since the distinction made on this day will carry such weight, we would be wise to understand the criteria the Shepherd will use when making His declaration. As a judge presiding over a case examines all of the evidence before issuing his verdict, so the Shepherd will examine all the evidence of one's life before handing down His final verdict. As we have seen in the previous two parables, there is always visible evidence that is produced from an invisible source. There are actions and attitudes that flow outward from deep within the heart, which serve as concrete evidence of the type of heart that resides within. In short, one's actions reveal the condition of one's heart. When one comes to Christ for salvation, his heart is forever changed, which inevitably leads to a transformed life.

In this illustration, Jesus provided several examples of the outward actions that will reveal the inner heart. He talked about such things as providing a meal to someone who is hungry, giving a drink to someone who is thirsty, inviting a stranger into one's home, clothing a person in need, caring for someone who is sick, and visiting a fellow believer who is in prison. These were everyday actions that demonstrated an extraordinary love for God. It was not that the action itself would gain them access to heavenly rewards. No one could ever earn their own salvation (Eph. 2:8–9). A person's actions do, however, reveal the condition of his heart. In this case, there was sufficient evidence that their hearts were aligned with the heart of Christ. In fact, Christ declared that their care and concern for others was an outgrowth of their care and concern for Him. He stated, *"I tell you the truth, whatever you did for one of the least of these brothers of mine, you did for me"* (Mt. 25:40).

For the other group—the goats on the Shepherd's left—the absence of this care and concern for others is what Christ will use as evidence of their lack of care and concern for Him. He said to them, *"I tell you the truth, whatever you did not do for one of the least of these, you did not do for me"* (Mt. 25:45). The heart that lacks love for others demonstrates a lack of love for Christ. Elsewhere in the Bible, a person who claims that he loves God when he lacks love for others is labeled a liar (1 Jn. 4:19–21). In Matthew 7:21, Jesus warned that *"not everyone who says to me, 'Lord, Lord' will enter the kingdom of heaven, but only he who does the will of my Father who is in heaven."* Genuine salvation creates a heart for the things that matter most to God.

Believers in Christ display spiritual fruit in their lives, which identifies them as unmistakably belonging to Christ. The Bible refers to this evidence as the fruit of the Spirit (Gal. 5:16–25). It consists of love, joy, peace, patience, kindness, goodness, faithfulness, gentleness, and self-control. People who have been reborn will strive to love God with all their heart, with all their soul, and with all their mind, and they will love their neighbor as they love themselves (Mt. 22:37–39).

Each of us should begin by examining our own lives. If all we can produce as evidence that we belong to Christ is a church membership card, a baptism certificate, or a receipt of a charitable donation, we had better reexamine our relationship with Christ to ensure that it is genuine. A real relationship with Christ produces unmistakable fruit, and plenty of it. When Christ is made the Lord of a person's life, there is a transformation that always takes place. In a very real sense, that life is placed "Under New

Management!" because God has moved in. When God moves into a life, He changes it from the inside out.

How do you know if your faith is genuine? Ask yourself, "Does the faith that I profess affect the way I live my life? Does it impact my decisions? Does it enrich my relationships? Does it create in me a hunger for the things that are foremost on the heart of God?" If not, something is seriously missing, and the time to "work out your salvation with fear and trembling" is now, not later.

We have a God who created us and loves us more than we could ever imagine. His desire is not for us to spend another moment separated from Him, but to spend the rest of our lives with Him experiencing all that He has created for our enjoyment.

Three times, in short succession, Jesus told His disciples He would be returning for those who genuinely belong to Him. He warned them to prepare themselves as a bride who was anxiously waiting for her groom. He demonstrated the importance of living as faithful stewards of all that God had entrusted to their care. And finally, He explained that He expected His followers to demonstrate their love for Him by loving those around them.

In all three lessons, we are reminded that our deeds in this life reveal the type of heart that resides within each of us. In all three lessons, we are reminded that the condition of our heart will have eternal implications. And in all three lessons, we are reminded that once Christ returns our fate will be sealed, with no chance to "try again."

It is very misleading, inaccurate, and downright dangerous for teachers of the Bible to insinuate that if a person is unprepared when Christ returns they will be given further opportunities to repent and get things right. Everything Jesus says in these three parables speaks to the contrary. To teach something other than what Christ teaches concerning our need to be prepared for His imminent return is deceptive, and it runs the risk of setting people up to be eternally separated from Christ.

SECTION THREE

THE FIRST WAVE

Having familiarized ourselves with Jesus' words concerning the end-times, it is now time to turn our attention to what the Bible reveals in the book of Revelation concerning the last days. We must use the map that Jesus presented to His disciples to guide us through the mountain of material that awaits us. I will seek to blend the two together as we proceed forward.

There is no need to be fearful of this book of the Bible. It was given to help prepare us for what is sure to come. One thing is for certain: God will carry out the events of the final days according to the exit strategy He designed before the creation of the world. Things will progress exactly as He has promised. What I *want* to occur, and what I *think* will occur, matter very little in God's plan. My job is not to set the agenda for the final days; it is to prepare myself for what God has promised will take place. To help each of us get ready, God revealed to John many of the details concerning that time in human history. John recorded what God revealed to him in the final book of the Bible—Revelation.

Instead of simply listing for John the events that were set to occur, God invited John to watch as God's plan was acted out like a drama unfolding before him. To use a military image, John was carried to the theatre of operations where he could witness the events of the future acted out before him. John recorded the details of each scene as they were portrayed on the stage of Heaven. Some of the dramatic scenes occurred on the earth while other portions simultaneously occurred in the heavens. These dual-stage dramas would make it difficult for us to establish a meaningful timeline of events without the help of the map Jesus provided.

This is where my book will differ from many other books on this subject. I start with what Jesus taught about the second coming and allow the other biblical writers to fill in the details. Many other authors create their timeline based upon a chronological reading of the Revelation text and then try to manipulate the words of Christ to fit their conclusions.

In order to correctly interpret the message of the book of Revelation, we must recognize that the type of language used in this particular book of the Bible is different from the language used in much of the rest of the Bible. John's language is apocalyptic in nature. By definition, that type of language is very symbolic. Thus, we are required to interpret it differently than we would other types of literature. Just as you would read a poem differently than a legal document, so also the contents of the book of Revelation must be read differently than other parts of the Bible. This is not being irresponsible with the text; rather it is interpreting it just as it was meant to be interpreted.

Because of the nature of John's writing, trying to force a literal interpretation of each of the elements of the book of Revelation does not make sense. The imagery that John used was never meant to be interpreted literally. However, when one begins to interpret symbolic literature, if he is not careful, he can make the literature say just about anything he wants it to say. Great caution must be taken to make sure that is not done. This is one other reason it is so critical to begin with the map that Jesus provided. His map sketches out the events, while John's descriptions provide the colorful details.

The symbolism contained throughout the drama must be understood in light of the time in which John lived. It must have proven difficult for John to describe events that were set to happen thousands of years into the future with the limited knowledge and vocabulary he and his peers possessed. Imagine trying to describe a flat-panel plasma television to someone who had never heard of electricity. How would you describe this television that hangs on the wall of your home through which you can see live images from around the world? Imagine trying to explain a modern-day war to someone living two thousand years ago. What images and words would you use to describe an airplane, a bomb, a drone, or a heat-seeking missile to someone who could not imagine anything larger than an eagle flying through the air? Even if someone had provided you with the name of each of those things, how would any of your listeners understand what you were describing?

You see, God could have provided John with the exact names and descriptions of all the instruments He would use to bring about the end, but those things would have proven meaningless to everyone living prior to the day they were unveiled. So, instead of just furnishing John a list of end-time events, God invited John to view a series of dramas that spelled out what those events would look like. John used colorful metaphors and similes to describe what he witnessed.

All of these things make the book of Revelation a challenge to interpret, but with the help of the Holy Spirit it is not as difficult as you might think.

CHAPTER EIGHT

PREPARING FOR DEPLOYMENT

John began the book of Revelation with the following words: *"The revelation of Jesus Christ, which God gave him to show his servants what must soon take place. He made it known by sending his angel to his servant John, who testifies to everything he saw—that is, the word of God and the testimony of Jesus Christ"* (Rev. 1:1–2). From these two verses we learn several important facts. The book was written to reveal Jesus and His future activities. He is the central figure. The message originated with God, and it was given to His followers. The book's purpose was to prepare God's servants for all that would occur before Christ's return. God used angels and other heavenly creatures to help make known His message to John, who faithfully recorded everything he was shown by God.

John wrote this book from the small island of Patmos (Rev. 1:9), where it is believed he had been exiled as a result of his faith in Christ. John divided the contents of his letter into two sections. Understanding this division is critical to understanding John's complete message. John was told, *"Write, therefore, what you have seen, what is now and what will take place later"* (Rev. 1:19). In that statement, we are told that part of John's message addressed the day in which he was living—*"what is now."* The other part of his message addressed a time that was yet to come—*"what will take place later."* This division of the text takes place very naturally between chapters three and four.

Chapters two and three contain instructions from Jesus to seven churches scattered across the province of Asia in John's day (Rev. 1:4). Jesus had a personal message for each of these churches, which He communicated through John. While Jesus' messages to those churches spoke directly to each of the churches of that day, they have also proven applicable to churches of all ages. Since the focus of this book is on the things concerning the end of time, I am going to refrain from discussing in detail the content of the letters to the seven churches. Instead I will focus on the things that *"will take place later."* It is not that the contents of the letters to these seven churches are not timely or valuable; they are both. It is simply that they are outside the scope of this book.

With the beginning of chapter four, the content of John's message shifted from the *"now"* of John's day to the *"what will take place later."* At this point, John made the intentional transition that he announced in chapter one. As mentioned earlier, those who hold to a pretribulational view of the rapture try to insert the rapture of the Church at this point in John's narrative. Their grounds for making this arbitrary insertion rest upon their claim that John does not specifically mention the Church again after chapter three. Their argument is invalid.

Throughout the whole book of Revelation John *was* writing to the Church—the servants of God—who would be required to endure the things that *"will take place later."* He was writing to prepare them for the things he was about to mention. He did not even hint that the rapture might occur at this point. He simply transitioned from the discussion concerning the churches of his day to a discussion of the Church of the future. John signaled this transition when he recorded, *"The voice I had first heard speaking to me like a trumpet said, 'Come up here, and I will show you what must take place after this'"* (Rev. 4:1). There was to be no mistake that the message that followed was going to address the events leading up to the end of time.

The remainder of chapters four and five reveals the incredible worship service that John witnessed in Heaven. In this portion of the vision, Christ stepped forward, took the sealed scroll from His Father's hand, and prepared to make known the events of the final days.

From this portion of Scripture, we learn that the events of the end will begin the moment Christ initiates them—not a second sooner, or later. He is the only One, in all of Heaven or Earth, declared worthy of the honor of directing such events (Rev. 5:3–5). As a disciplined soldier would never fire the first shot without his commanding officer giving the order, so none of the events of the end will commence until Jesus gives the command.

When that time arrives, He will unveil that portion of history in the way, and at the pace, that God has ordained.

It is worth noting that none of these events will happen by coincidence. They will occur exactly as God has ordained for them to occur. This is incredibly important to remember because no matter how terrible things may seem, God will remain in complete control. Even when Satan is allowed to participate in the unfolding of these future events, he is only carrying out what God has ordained must occur. In essence, he (Satan) and his fallen foes are merely instruments in the hands of Almighty God. Their power is limited, and their ability to alter God's plan is nonexistent.

There are three main series of events through which John tells this incredible story: the seals, the trumpets, and the bowls. Each series contains seven elements with an interlude placed between the sixth and seventh elements of the first two series. These interludes serve several purposes in the text. First, they provide much-needed information for the ones who will be living through the events John is describing. Second, they show an incredible distinction in the final outcome of those who belong to God and those who do not. Third, they remind the suffering Church that God has an incredible plan designed just for it, and that its sufferings will pale in comparison to the glory He has in store for it. In short, these interludes provide hope in the midst of suffering—hope that believers will need in order to remain faithful to the end.

God unfolds the events of the seals and trumpets according to a specific pattern, or rhythm, as a poet might lay out a poem. Both series begin with the introduction of four events that occur back-to-back with little additional explanation as to their meaning. These are followed by two more detailed events. Then, an interlude of hope is introduced. And finally, the seventh element of each series is included as a transition leading to the next series.

While the rhythm of the seals and trumpets is similar, the two series also present a couple of stark contrasts. The suffering mentioned in the first four seals seems to be of a human origin, while the suffering mentioned in the first four trumpets is of a natural or supernatural origin. The suffering also seems to intensify as John moves from the seal series to the trumpet series.

While the series of bowl judgments do not follow the same rhythmic pattern as the seals and the trumpets, the bowl judgments are very similar to the trumpets in their content. The trumpets reveal massive, but limited destruction, while the bowl judgments bring about complete destruction. All of this will be explained in greater detail as we progress through the book.

Let us now turn our attention to the events God revealed would occur in those final days. You will certainly see how closely they follow the map that Jesus laid out for His disciples.

CHAPTER NINE
STAGING

In the military, as a campaign is about to get underway, the elements needed to assure victory are all moved into place. Ships, planes, tanks, ammunition, supply lines, and personnel are all stationed in strategic locations from which they will be able to launch their attack. This is known as "staging." In some ways, this is what John is about to be shown.

To describe the first four seals, John used the imagery of four horsemen, all riding different color horses, acting out their parts of the end-time drama. Jesus referred to the events occurring during this time period as *"the beginning of birth pains"* (Mt. 24:8). As the events of the end unfold, in many ways they will resemble a woman progressing through childbirth. For most women, the contractions (birth pains) start off mild and are spaced out over time. As labor progresses, and the time of birth draws near, the contractions greatly increase in intensity and in frequency. We will see this unfold as John describes the events of the end. The onset of these events will begin gradually, but as the time draws near for Christ to return, they are sure to increase in their intensity and their frequency. John's message closely follows Jesus' metaphor.

Seal One (Rev. 6:1–2)

Christ, having received the scroll from His Father, served as the leader of the divine drama. As He broke open the first seal, He functioned like a director on a movie set screaming, "Action!" At Christ's command, the first scene is acted out before John's eyes. In this scene, a rider on a white horse is ordered to come forth. Immediately, on cue, the rider and the horse appear. The rider is seen holding a bow and wearing a crown that he had been given. He rode out *"as a conqueror bent on conquest"* (Rev. 6:1–2).

From this short scene we learn that Christ is in complete control of the drama. He calls all of the shots. Every actor in the divine drama is under His control and His leadership. Nothing can happen without His permission. This will be the case for each of the events that are set to unfold.

The imagery John used to describe this first seal vision would have been familiar to his first-century audience. Most of his readers would have understood that the bow was a symbol of military might and conquest. They had probably witnessed victorious military generals being awarded the victor's crown by the one who wore the royal crown. In the Roman world, it was extremely common for the victorious military general to celebrate his victory by parading through the streets of Rome riding on a white horse, or riding in a chariot drawn by white horses. In this parade, he would lead his army, humiliate his captives, and display all of the bounty he had gained for his king. It was viewed as the ultimate display of victory.

Through this brief scene we are given a glimpse of a leader returning from battle, to be celebrated and rewarded for having conquered his foe. We are not told the identity of the victor, nor the enemy he has defeated. We are not told what type of battle he has won, whether it is a military, physical, political, or philosophical battle. He is simply pictured as the victor.

While it cannot be known for certain, it is likely that John was indicating that the turmoil of the end will be preceded by a time of peace brought about by some type of conquest. The victor will be celebrated as having brought about the peace, but this peace will not last. John hints to that fact when he describes the victor as a *"conqueror bent on conquest"* (Rev. 1:2). This alerts the reader that he is not finished conquering. While it is likely that many in that day will think lasting peace has been achieved, the seals, which follow, demonstrate that it has not.

Much debate has been waged over whether this victor is an actual person, or simply some type of worldwide peace movement. While we cannot be absolutely sure, the context seems to point toward some type of "movement" that promises peace. I say this because the next three horsemen symbolize war, famine, and death, and not individuals. It would seem consistent to view all four horsemen the same. Either way, a sense of false peace will be promised to the world during this initial phase of the end. Jesus warned His followers of those who would proclaim themselves to be peace-givers when He said, *"Watch out that no one deceives you. For many will come in my name, claiming 'I am the Christ' and will deceive many"* (Mt. 24:5). Jesus is the only Prince of Peace, but other people, or philosophies, will claim that they have found the keys to lasting peace. They are wrong!

Notice how subtle the events of the end will begin. Most unsuspecting people will not even know that the end is drawing near. That is exactly what Jesus and Paul said would happen (Mt. 24:37; 1 Thess. 5:3).

According to what Jesus told His disciples, many false claims will be made by those who wish to lead others astray (Mt. 24:4–5). We should not be fooled by their hollow promises of peace, or by their charismatic charm. Movements that promise peace are very seductive. After all, who would not enjoy living in a peaceful world?

It is the clear teaching of the Bible that genuine, lasting peace will not be achieved until the true Prince of Peace rules in all of His glory. Any promise of peace before that time is temporary at best.

Seal Two (Rev. 6:3–4)

With the drama of the first seal acted out, Jesus breaks open the second seal and the next actor is called onto the stage. Another horse and rider appear. This time the horse is colored a fiery red. *"Its rider was given power to take peace from the earth and to make men slay each other. To him was given a large sword"* (Rev. 6:4).

Here, John demonstrated that the celebration of peace would give way to cries of war. While the type of war is unclear, John indicated that it would be a global war by stating that the rider would be given the power to *"take peace from the earth."* During this war, men will slay one another on a grand scale.

John reported that the rider would be given a "large sword." John was not speaking of an actual "large sword." It was simply a phrase used to describe the extent of the war. In fact, the word that John chose for "sword" referred to a small sword that a soldier, or an assassin, would carry into battle. Instead, the phrase "large sword" was chosen to indicate the widespread nature of the conflict and the amount of damage that the war will inflict. He was communicating that it would be a large war, as peace vanishes and men begin to slaughter one another.

This war will follow closely on the heels of the false peace just as Jesus had warned. He said, *"You will hear of wars and rumors of wars, but see to it that you are not alarmed. Such things must happen, but the end is still to come. Nation will rise against nation, and kingdom against kingdom"* (Mt. 24:6–7). This war will not be what you might expect. If I understand what Jesus is saying, this war will be fought for religious reasons. When Jesus said "nation will rise against nation" the term He used for nation was the term *ethnos* from which we get our word ethnic. He was saying that this war will pit one "ethnos" against another "ethnos." This description would encompass differing religious groups fighting one another. It would be similar to a holy war, or a jihad. This could occur if one religion (or nonreligion) decided to impose its beliefs on the rest of the world and eliminate anyone who was a nonsupporter. This type of scenario fits the rest of the book of Revelation perfectly.

Seal Three (Rev. 6:5–6)

As war swept across the face of the land, bringing an end to the short-lived false peace, another horse and rider are called forth on Jesus' cue. This time John reported, *"I looked, and there before me was a black horse! Its rider was holding a pair of scales in his hand. Then I heard what sounded like a voice among the four living creatures, saying, 'A quart of wheat for a day's wages, and three quarts of barley for a day's wages, and do not damage the oil and wine!'"* (Rev. 6:5–6).

This portion of the drama depicts a great famine and/or economic collapse that will follow on the heels of the war. The scales in the rider's hand represent the rationing of food that will take place in that day. In several places in the Old Testament, the people are reported to have "eaten bread by weight" due to the wrath of God being poured out against them (Lev. 26:26; Ezek. 4:16–17). The shortage of food will likely be brought on by the devastation of the war, which he has just introduced. You will remember that Jesus had mentioned the coming of these famines when He instructed His disciples (Mt. 24:7). This shortage of food will cause the price of food to be greatly inflated to the point that the average person will not be able to feed his family as he once did.

John describes the inflation this way: *"A quart of wheat for a day's wages, and three quarts of barley for a day's wages"* (Rev. 6:6). Wheat was a staple item in John's day. On the average, a working man would consume a quart of wheat each day. Here, John reveals that it will take all that an average man earns for a full day's work just to buy enough food for him to eat. That would leave nothing for the members of his family to eat. Before the great inflation of that day an average man's daily wages would buy eight times that much food.

A less expensive alternative would be the purchase of barley, which was cheaper, but of very low nutritional value. If a man chose to buy barley instead of wheat, he could secure three daily portions with the money he earned from working all day. This would allow him, his wife, and a child to eat, but they would have no money left to purchase any of their other necessities. A famine of this magnitude would cause the rest of the economy to suffer and eventually collapse.

One other interesting twist is added to this drama. Those buying the wheat and barley are ordered *"not to damage the oil and wine"* (Rev. 6:6). These items could only be afforded by the very wealthy during a time of famine. It could be that John was indicating that the wealthy, who could afford oil and wine, would be the ones selling the bare necessities to everyone else at exorbitant prices while hording the finer things of life for their own pleasures. This statement might also indicate that the government will have taken over the distribution of the food in those days. If that were the case, the government leaders would live in luxury while their people lived in sub-poverty conditions. Regardless of who would be selling the food in that day, John made it clear that the time of famine will be severe.

Seal Four (Rev. 6:7–8)

With three of the four horsemen having cleared the stage, Christ breaks the fourth seal and the final horse and rider are called to appear. This time, John reported that the horse was pale in color—literally "ashen"—like the face of one stricken with terror. The phrase "white as a ghost" comes to mind. The rider of this horse had been given a name: Death. Unlike the other three horsemen, this one had someone following close behind him. His name was Hades. John was told that these two *"were given power over a fourth of the earth to kill by sword, famine and plague, and by the wild beasts of the earth"* (Rev. 6:8).

This portion of the drama flows naturally from the previous three. False peace gave way to war. War led to famine. Now, famine played a part in the death of humanity on a massive scale.

The rider of the pale horse was named Death, and Hades (the grave) was close behind. Death and Hades were allowed by Christ to claim the lives of one-fourth of the world's population. At the world's current population of six billion people, that would represent roughly 1.5 billion deaths occurring in a very short time. Lives will be extinguished *"by sword, famine, and plague, and by the wild beasts of the earth"* (Rev. 6:8). While John had mentioned the devastation of the sword and famine in the previous sections, two new instruments of death are added: plagues and wild beasts of the earth. It is understandable that as the famine spread and people were unable to get proper nutrition, their bodies would become more susceptible to plagues. The wild beasts would also be lacking food and would turn on the weak individuals and devour them.

Ezekiel had used this same combination to describe the coming judgment of God upon an unfaithful people in the Old Testament. Ezekiel recorded the warning God had issued in his day: *"For this is what the Sovereign LORD says: How much worse will it be when I send against Jerusalem my four dreadful judgments—sword and famine and wild beasts and plague—to kill its men and their animals!"* (Ezek. 14:21). John was witnessing an event reminiscent of Ezekiel's day.

Those living in that day without biblical understanding may simply see these events as another dark day in human history, but students of God's Word will recognize it as a reminder that the time is drawing near for Christ to return and claim those who belong to Him.

With this, the curtain closed on the dramas of the four horsemen. Yet, Jesus was not finished revealing to John all that would occur. He was just warming up. There was more yet to come.

CHAPTER TEN

FIELD REPORT

Following the four horsemen, the scene shifted from events occurring on earth, to a conversation that took place in Heaven. What John saw and heard next, no human had ever witnessed before. By breaking the fifth seal, Jesus called for the curtain to open and the next scene to commence.

Seal Five (Rev. 6:9–11)

John must have been in awe of what he witnessed next. He saw *"under the altar the souls of those who had been slain because of the word of God and the testimony they had maintained"* (Rev. 6:9). Imagine seeing the souls of those who had been martyred for refusing to compromise their faith in God. These are those faithful saints who refused to compromise their faith in order to save their lives. They had willingly laid down their lives in order to follow Christ.

Jesus had spoken of this level of sacrifice when he warned, *"You will be handed over to be persecuted and put to death, and you will be hated by all nations because of me"* (Mt. 24:9). Mark and Luke both reported that during this time of great martyrdom Christians would be witnesses for God to governors and kings, and these believers would be empowered by the Holy Spirit to speak words of wisdom that none of their adversaries would be able to resist or contradict (Mk. 13:9–13; Lk. 21:12–15).

The fact that John saw the souls of these individuals under the altar lets us know that they had not been exempt from the unimaginable suffering the enemies of God had inflicted on them due to their faith in Christ. They had been privileged enough to accomplish God's purpose through their sufferings. Now that their mission on earth was over, and their suffering had ended, they were in Heaven in the presence of God. This assurance would become incredibly important to those who would follow behind them, especially as they faced persecutions of their own.

Through this scene, John learned that death was not to be feared. A Christian's greatest enemy is not death; it is apostasy. Dying for the cause of Christ is not to be viewed as some type of punishment; instead, it should be considered the highest honor afforded a follower of Christ.

John reported that the souls of those who had been slain were seen *"under the altar"* (Rev. 6:9). The altar to which John referred was not on Earth, but in Heaven. In fact, we are told in Hebrews that the earthly sanctuary was merely a *"copy and a shadow of what is in heaven"* (Heb. 8:5). The sacrifice that was offered on the heavenly altar was not the blood of a goat or a calf. Jesus Christ offered Himself and His own blood upon the heavenly altar. He was the only sacrifice that was acceptable (Heb. 9:11–28). For the Jew, the most sacred part of the sacrifice was the blood that was shed because it represented the very life of the one being sacrificed (Lev. 17:11–14). The blood of the sacrifice was collected and then poured out at the base of the altar (Lev. 4:7). This is the very place where John saw the souls of the martyrs.

This imagery would imply two things. First, Christ's blood, offered on that altar, was their covering. His blood had "cleansed their consciences from acts that lead to death," and His blood had granted them access into God's presence (Heb. 9:14). Second, the martyrs had willingly offered themselves as *"living sacrifices, holy and pleasing to God,"* which was their *"spiritual act of worship"* (Rom. 12:1). Even though their life blood could not save their souls, they had, nonetheless, offered all they had to God in response to the tremendous sacrifice He had made on their behalf.

John tells us that the martyrs *"called out in a loud voice, 'How long, Sovereign Lord, holy and true, until you judge the inhabitants of the earth and avenge our blood?'"* (Rev. 6:10). They were not crying for vengeance, as if that would somehow make them feel better. They were acknowledging the sovereignty of their holy and true God. They were anxious to witness the promises of God being fulfilled. They had confidence that God would set all things right. They simply wanted to know when it would occur.

Notice God's two-part response to their inquiry. John reported, *"Then each of them was given a white robe, and they were told to wait a little longer, until the number of their fellow servants and brothers who were to be killed as they had been was completed"* (Rev. 6:11). First, they were clothed with a white robe, symbolizing their victory and purity in Christ. These would not have been literal robes, as the resurrection of their bodies had not yet occurred. God was, however, showing John that they had been made pure by the blood of Christ. Then, God informed those under the altar that they would have to wait a little longer until His plan had been completely carried out—a plan that would include the martyrdom of many other believers. His response satisfied them as they knew He was sovereign, holy, and true to His promise.

CHAPTER ELEVEN
SHOCK AND AWE

As the curtain fell on the previous scene in Heaven, Jesus stepped forward to announce the beginning of another scene, which would occur back on earth. What John witnessed in the next few moments encapsulated every terror that the people of his day could have imagined. Since the times of the Old Testament, Jews had always associated the destruction of the earth and cosmic upheaval with the end of time.

Seal Six (Rev. 6:12–17)

As the sixth seal was cracked opened, John witnessed five incredible events that struck fear in the hearts of the inhabitants of the earth. The first event was a great earthquake. Next, he described noticeable changes to the sun and the moon, as the sun turned black and the moon turned blood red. Then, as if the sky itself were being shaken, John watched as the stars of the sky fell to the earth. Next, he witnessed the rolling up of the sky like a scroll. And finally, he noted the dislodgment of the mountains and islands from their places. Events of a similar nature had long since been predicted by the Old Testament prophets, as well as Jesus. John watched in amazement as they took place before his eyes.

Many opinions have been offered as to the exact nature of each of these events. Some have tried to compare John's descriptions with modern-day equivalents. Most try to equate John's description to a nuclear war. While that could be the case, such speculation is not profitable. The fact is, God could execute this part of His plan exactly as it is described—simply by ordering the cosmos to do what He commands. That is not to say that He will not achieve His goal through some type of modern warfare. He could do that as well. The method of the destruction is not important. What is worth noting is that God will use these events to get the attention of mankind, calling them to repent before it is too late. Some will heed His warning, and others will not.

Regardless of their status or rank (kings, princes, generals, rich, mighty, slave, or free), John noted that the inhabitants of the earth were all stricken with fear. Every one of them ran and hid in caves and among the rocks of the mountains. They pleaded for the rocks to fall on them and hide them from *"the face of him who sits on the throne and from the wrath of the lamb"* (Rev. 6:15–16). These inhabitants knew that death would be better than having to face the wrath of God unprepared. Evidently many of them understood that they were living in the great day of God's wrath, and with that understanding came the realization that they were not prepared to stand (Rev. 6:17).

While one might argue that there is no sign of repentance in their words or actions, there does seem to be a hint of conviction. They suddenly realized they were in no condition to meet God face to face. They wanted to know if there was any hope for them. John heard someone ask, "Can anyone stand in the great day of God's wrath?" If so, who? That was a question God was about to answer.

CHAPTER TWELVE

BULLET-PROOF BUNKER GEAR

With the closing of the curtain on seal six, John was shown a two-part vision, which would serve as an interlude in this series. Some have argued that this scene is out of place in the drama. They claim it interrupts the flow of the revelation God was making known to John. However, that is not the case at all. What was about to be revealed to John was needed at precisely this moment.

As this living parable was acted out before John, it supplied the answer to the final question posed in seal six (Rev. 6:17), and it provided the hope believers would need to remain faithful to the end. Had this information come earlier, it would not have been understood, and had it come later it might not have been as effective.

Those living through the events of the end would need this information in order to hold on. It would serve as a type of double-layered body armor. The first layer will provide the protection and the second layer will add the comfort. Both of these would be needed as things got tougher.

Layer One: Shield of Ownership (Rev. 7:1-8)

Contrary to the opinion that this scene is out of place, it actually flows directly out of the sixth seal. At the end of the sixth seal, we are told that the inhabitants of the earth are panic stricken due to seeing the *"face of him who sits on the throne"* and the *"Lamb"* (Rev. 6:16). Then, John hears the inhabitants of the earth asking the question, "Who can stand?" John is about to be given the answer to that question.

This living parable was acted out in two parts. The first half was a snapshot of a life-changing event that took place on earth. The second half of the story showed the impact the event had on eternity.

As the first part unfolded, four angels were introduced who were ordered to restrain the harmful winds from blowing across the earth. To understand this imagery, one must recognize that at this time in history it was the common belief that the world was flat. Winds that came from the four points of a compass were considered favorable winds (north, south, east, and west). Winds that originated at the four corners of the earth and blew diagonally across the land were considered to be destructive. So, in this scene the angels overseeing the damaging winds are ordered to keep those winds from wreaking havoc on the earth while a fifth angel completed his assignment from God.

As the harmful winds were restrained, a fifth angel came from the east (the direction symbolic of salvation) with the seal of the living God in his possession. He was to use the seal to clearly mark, or identify, all those who belonged to God. In that day, a king's seal served to mark ownership of something, and it guaranteed security for the particular item (or person) that bore his seal. In this case, John was told that the seal was to be used to mark those servants who belonged to the living God.

The seal (mark of ownership) was to be placed on their foreheads—one way of saying it would be in plain sight of all whom they would meet. There would be no "camouflage Christians" content on blending in with the world. There would be none who were ashamed to be known as one of His followers. This seal would unmistakably identify them as belonging to God. It would also identify them as enemies of the evil one. It was a stark contrast to the mark of the beast, which the followers of the antichrist would later receive.

What was this seal? While we cannot be certain, other portions of Scripture refer to the seal of God being the indwelling of the Holy Spirit. Notice what Paul had to say about this subject. Paul spoke of the sealing of believers when he wrote: *"Now it is God who makes both us and you stand firm in Christ. He anointed us, set his seal of ownership on us, and put his Spirit in our hearts as a deposit, guaranteeing what is to come"* (2 Cor. 1:21–22). He repeated this truth in Ephesians where he wrote: *"And you also were included in Christ when you heard the word of truth, the gospel of your salvation. Having believed, you were marked in him with a seal, the promised Holy Spirit, who is a deposit guaranteeing our inheritance until the redemption of those who are God's possession—to the praise of his glory"* (Eph. 1:13–14). When an individual comes to faith in Christ, he or she is sealed with the Holy Spirit, identifying that person as one belonging to God. This interlude is a vivid reminder of how important the indwelling of the Holy Spirit will be in those days. Those who lack His presence will not be able to stand in the midst of great persecution. In the end, it is what distinguishes a true believer from the pretender.

The sealing of the followers of God served to answer the question posed at the end of seal six. Do you remember that question? Those enduring the sixth seal wanted to know, who will be able to stand when the wrath of God is poured out? The answer: only those who have been sealed by God—filled by His Holy Spirit. Only those who belong to Him! No one else will be able to stand. This seal will provide them the protection they will need during the events that come later. While Christians will not be removed from the battlefield, they will be protected.

There has been much disagreement surrounding the identity of the individuals referenced in this portion of Scripture. Some people, mainly those influenced by dispensationalism, insist that the 144,000 people mentioned in the first scene are the Jews that will be "automatically" saved by God at this particular point in time. They cite the eleventh chapter of Romans to support their claim. They say that since John listed the twelve tribes of Israel individually, and mentioned a specific number of people as being marked, it must mean that God, in His sovereignty, suddenly claimed these people as His own, as if they were unable to resist His offer of salvation. This event, they claim, must be the great ingathering of the Jews that they teach will occur during the tribulation. However, that is not what this story was promising, nor is it what Paul promised in Romans chapter eleven.

While it is true that the group, which was sealed, was said to have come from "all the tribes of Israel," that phrase does not necessarily have to mean that he was speaking of those with a Jewish bloodline. Follow me on this one. In the second chapter of Ephesians, Paul makes it explicitly clear that the Gentiles who were once *"separate from Christ, excluded from citizenship in*

Israel and foreigners to the covenants of the promise" have been made *"fellow citizens with God's people and members of God's household"* through the reconciling work of Christ on the cross (Eph. 2:11–22). Paul was stating that even though the Gentiles had not been allowed to participate in the Mosaic covenant, which God made with the Jews on Mount Sinai, they had been included in the new covenant that God established through Christ's work on the cross. This fact is undeniable based upon the explicit teachings of God's Word. Paul also made it clear that Christ abolished the *"law with its commandments and regulations"* (the old covenant) for the purpose of *"creating one new man out of the two, thus making peace, and in this one body to reconcile both of them to God through the cross, by which he put to death their hostility"* (Eph. 2:14–16).

Paul did say in the eleventh chapter of Romans that God was able to graft the Jews back into His spiritual vine *"if they did not persist in their unbelief"* (Rom. 11:23). In this passage, Paul clearly teaches that if the Jews come to faith, they must come as every other believer comes—by faith in Jesus Christ. No doubt some of those "marked" in this Revelation passage are from a Jewish background, but not all of them should be viewed in that light. There is no doubt that many who possess a Jewish bloodline will have their spiritual eyes opened during the final days, resulting in a great harvest of souls. That day will surely come. However, that is not the message of the first half of this story.

Another indicator that John did not intend for his readers to interpret his message to mean that he was only referring to Jews of the old covenant can be seen in the fact that his list of the twelve tribes of Israel does not match any of the lists found elsewhere in the Bible. A close look at John's list reveals that two of the twelve original tribes (Dan and Ephraim) are missing altogether from the list. Both of these tribes are well known for their involvement with idolatry. Their omission is an indicator that the wicked will not be included in the group that makes up God's chosen few, even if they possess a Jewish bloodline.

Those who invest countless hours insisting that God will somehow re-gather and seal 12,000 individuals from each of the twelve tribes of Israel, ignore the fact that several of those tribes are extinct, and two of them were not even included in John's list. While it is true that God can do anything He desires, those who insist on this exclusive ingathering of Jews are missing the whole point of John's message. This is not about twelve literal tribes of the old covenant being drafted into God's army. The purpose of this entire interlude was to assure those who belonged to God that He knew who they were, and that He had plans for their future. In other words, they had not been forgotten despite what their circumstances might otherwise indicate.

In the second half of this interlude, John refers to this group as *"a great multitude that no one could count, from every nation, tribe, people and language"* (Rev. 7:9). The first half of the story cannot be separated from the second half. They must be interpreted as a unit, just as John presented them to his readers.

God's protection and ownership will not be extended to people based upon their bloodline or lineage (Jew or Gentile). It will be extended to all who come to Him through faith in Christ—to all who bear the mark of His seal.

Rather than suggesting that all the Jews are simultaneously converted at this point, John is simply stating that all who belong to God will bear His mark upon their lives. This mark will be the proof that they belong to Him, and proof that they will enjoy His eternal protection. He was sealing them with the undeniable mark of His Spirit, claiming them as His own and guaranteeing them of their future with Him. Not one of them will be forsaken by God.

Layer Two: The Comfort of Knowing the Joy That Awaits (Rev. 7:9-17)

In the second half of this interlude, the scene shifted from Earth back to Heaven. The effect of what had been done on Earth (the sealing of God's people) was about to be seen in Heaven. On Heaven's stage, John witnessed a worship service that was meant to encourage him and all who would face the terrible times of tribulation ahead. The great multitude of worshipers who were gathered around God's throne were from *"every nation, tribe, people and language,"* and their number was too numerous for John to count (Rev. 7:9). Notice that their number was not limited to 144,000 nor was their ancestry exclusively Jewish. They were joined by many other believers.

They were seen celebrating before God's throne clothed in white robes and holding palm branches in their hands (Rev. 7:9). Their white robes symbolize their purity in Christ, and John later reveals that the white robes represent the righteous deeds of the saints (Rev. 19:8). The palm branches were symbolic of the great joy that filled their hearts.

These believers had reason to celebrate. God had brought them through the times of tribulation successfully. They were victorious over Satan. Even though Satan appeared victorious when he took their lives, they ended up victorious in the end because they belonged to God.

When asked if he knew who these people were and where they came from, John politely declined to attempt an answer. After a moment of hesitation, the question was answered by the one who had asked it. He said to John, *"These are they who have come out of the great tribulation; they have washed their robes and made them white in the blood of the Lamb"* (Rev. 7:14). John was told that they were servants at God's throne, and never again would they suffer as they once did on earth (Rev. 7:15–17).

You may ask why this information would be critical for John and his readers at this point. Several reasons could be supplied. First, all believers would need to know that no distinction was going to be made between Jewish and Gentile Christians as they served before God's throne. Jews and Gentiles are together there, and they will make up the multitude from all nations, tribes, peoples, and languages that will worship and serve in the presence of God. Jews and Gentiles were not competing for a place at God's throne. There was room for everyone.

Second, all who were there had come through Christ, as was made clear through the statement that each person had washed white his or her robe in the blood of the Lamb.

Third, this knowledge would prove comforting and provide hope to John's audience, as many of them would lose their lives during days of great tribulation. John was offered the assurance that the Christians who died during the days of the great tribulation would be gathered around the throne of God for all eternity. This was to remain their hope throughout the most difficult days they would ever experience.

This interlude is about hope in the midst of suffering. It is about the assurance we have in Christ that no matter what Satan brings against us, as children of God we are secure. It is about the celebration that will occur as the whole family of God gathers around His throne and rejoices in the salvation that God has provided them in Christ. It is about an eternity where Christ will shepherd His sheep and never again will they be found in need. Those whom God seals, He saves—for ever and ever! Because He is faithful, we can live with our eyes on eternity! He is our hope!

CHAPTER THIRTEEN

A BRIEF CEASE-FIRE

Having completed the interlude, John's attention was, once again, directed toward the opening of the final seal. He must have been anticipating that God was about to wrap things up. Could things get any worse? Could there be any more devastation than what he had already witnessed? Those questions were soon to be answered.

Instead of the seventh seal wrapping things up, it seemed to merely open the door to another series of seven events that would follow. Some suggest that instead of being totally sequential (seven seals, followed by seven trumpets, followed by seven bowls) each new series was a part of the final event of the previous series. Perhaps a simple word picture would help to make this easier to understand.

It would be similar to taking a tour of a seven-story museum. The first floor would contain the items mentioned in seal one. The second floor would contain items mentioned in seal two, and so on. However, the seventh floor would be a little bit different. When exiting the elevator on the seventh floor, you would enter a lobby, where a brief description of the remainder of the tour is offered. Then, you would be shown seven doors, each of which would lead to another room. Room number one would contain the first trumpet. Room number two would contain the second trumpet, and so on. However, the seventh room would be a little different from the first six. This room is a room of contrasts. The north half is painted a glossy bright white; the south half is painted a flat black. The two sides are separated by a curtain similar to what you would find in a semi-private hospital room. The white side contains a window that is closed for a few more moments, but hanging above the window is a sign labeled "Reward and Celebration." (John will be allowed to look out this window a little bit later in Revelation, but for now it remained closed). The black side of the room is set up like a junior high science fair with seven individual displays depicting the seven bowls of God's wrath. Above the displays hangs a sign labeled "Judgment and Wrath." The speakers in the ceiling of that room carry the message contained in trumpet seven, explaining the distinct differences between the two sides of the room.

Without pushing this analogy too far, the seals would represent the seven floors of the building. The trumpets would be contained on the seventh floor, otherwise known as the "Seventh Seal Floor." And, then, the bowls would be contained within the room labeled "Trumpet Seven." All three series are contained in one building, yet they remain distinct.

Seal Seven (Rev. 8:1–5)

As the curtain rose on the seventh seal, in stark contrast to all of the noise of the sixth seal, there was a moment of silence throughout Heaven—about half an hour of silence. Oh, the suspense that must have built! It was like the quiet before a great storm. Eight actors walked out onto the stage and took their places.

Seven of the angels were each given a trumpet, which would be used later in the drama. Their presence on the stage must have alerted John that things were far from being over.

Then, an eighth angel appeared, holding a golden censer filled with incense to offer on the golden altar before the throne (Rev. 8:3). This altar was known as the altar of incense. It was the same altar under which John had seen the souls of the martyrs during the opening of the fifth seal (Rev. 6:9). It will also be referenced again in connection with the sixth trumpet (Rev. 9:13).

The angel offered to God much incense along with the prayers of the saints. John's theology would forbid interpreting that statement to mean that the angel served as some type of mediator between God and His people. Rather, this statement implied that as the prayers of God's people were being offered to God, the angel offered incense upon the golden altar. It was a common practice in that day to burn incense during prayer vigils.

It is interesting to note that when the saints of God prayed, all of Heaven grew silent as a gesture signifying that their prayers were being heard. Not only were their prayers being heard in Heaven, but God's response to those prayers would soon be felt on earth. The angel with the censer in his hand, *"filled it with fire from the altar, and hurled it on the earth"* (Rev. 8:5). With that act, the silence was officially over. *"Peals of thunder, rumblings, flashes of lightning, and an earthquake"* rocked the earth (Rev. 8:5). God was letting the inhabitants of the earth know that things were far from over.

The transition from the seals to the trumpets was underway. The trumpets had been distributed to the seven angels, and they were about to be sounded. Things were about to get very interesting. There was no time for John to take a bathroom break!

SECTION FOUR

THE SECOND WAVE

As we explore the seven trumpets, you will notice that the severity of the destruction is greater with the trumpets than it was with the seals. It is as if the birth pains are growing more and more intense as the world moves closer to its day of delivery. Jesus had warned that this would occur, and John is about to have that confirmed. Even though the destruction is increasing in its intensity, it still remains limited by God. He retains complete control. Nothing will happen without His permission.

God sounds these trumpets in order to get the attention of the inhabitants of the earth. He is warning them that the time is running out for them to make preparations for Christ's return. It is as if God is firing a warning shot to get the attention of His enemies, much like a captain of a battleship would fire a warning shot across the bow of an advancing enemy ship. These events were not meant to destroy His enemy, but to serve notice that God meant business.

Over the centuries, many writers have speculated as to the events leading up to the end and the instruments God would use to fulfill the scenes John was describing. After a recent visit to the World War II National Museum, I can certainly understand why those living in the 1940s must have thought they were living in the final days. It must have seemed that every element John linked to the end was occurring before their eyes. However, the return of Christ did not occur at that time. Evidently, the events of the end will be even worse than that terrible time in history. Who can even imagine something so horrific?

As to the instruments that God will use to bring about the end, many speculate that with the rapid proliferation of nuclear weapons, God could use them to wreak His havoc on the earth. However, one must not forget that God, who spoke the world into existence, could also destroy His creation simply by giving the order. When God speaks, things happen! So, while God may use man-made devices to bring about the disaster we are about to study, God is not limited by man's ability to destroy the earth. Instead of speculating about something that we have no way to prove, our time would be better spent exploring what the Bible does report and leaving the details up to God.

CHAPTER FOURTEEN

ENVIRONMENTAL DISASTER

Similar to the first four seals, the destruction created by the first four trumpets is introduced rapidly with few additional details supplied. It is also clothed in images familiar to the people of John's day.

Trumpet One (Rev. 8:7)

With the sounding of the first trumpet, *"hail and fire mixed with blood"* was hurled down upon the earth (Rev. 8:7). This language sounds familiar to the language used in the seventh seal. It served to link the two series together.

John reported the devastation that followed: *"A third of the earth was burned up, a third of the trees were burned up, and all the green grass was burned up"* (Rev. 8:7). Just that fast, massive devastation was doled out upon the earth. It is difficult to imagine a worldwide disaster of that magnitude, or the destruction that will be left in its path, but John said it would occur at the sounding of the first trumpet.

In our day, we have seen wildfires that have raged out of control for weeks, destroying thousands of miles of forest and hundreds of homes. The fire John described will put all other fires to shame. One-third of the entire earth will be scorched by the fires of the first trumpet. Imagine the devastation it will leave in its path.

By this point in time, those familiar with the Bible will have little doubt that the world is in the midst of its final days. Nothing this extreme would have ever happened before. The sad news is that things will get worse before they get better. God is just getting started. His divine warnings will intensify just like the ancient plagues on the land of Egypt intensified during the days of Moses.

In two short sentences, John described the destruction wrought by the first trumpet aimed at nature. It was then time to move on to the second trumpet.

Trumpet Two (Rev. 8:8–9)

With the sounding of the second trumpet, the second warning shot was fired from God's cannon. This time, John looked on as *"something like a huge mountain, all ablaze, was thrown into the sea"* (Rev. 8:8). The ensuing damage was that *"a third of the sea turned into blood, a third of the living creatures in the sea died, and a third of the ships were destroyed"* (Rev. 8:9). This time, the blast of destruction was aimed at the sea.

God, who created all sea life on the fifth day of creation, now destroys a third of it in one fell swoop. Try to imagine the massive clean-up effort that would have to be launched to contain the polluted water and to clean up the dead marine life. This says nothing about the massive rescue operation that would be initiated to search for the human lives shipwrecked at sea.

Again, the destruction would be dreadful, but still limited in its scope. This second trumpet is reminiscent of the first plague in Egypt when God struck the Nile River. It turned to blood, the fish in it died, and the water became undrinkable (Ex. 7:17–21). Even after such a demonstration of God's power, Pharaoh's heart was hardened. Something similar is sure to happen with many who are alive in these final days.

Once again, the mechanism of destruction cannot be completely understood. John simply described it as a huge mountain all ablaze. Whatever the instrument of destruction will be, its destructive potential will be incredible. What we are told about the effects of this trumpet is that one-third of the sea, the creatures in it, and the ships on it are destroyed. As well as inflicting physical damage to the earth, these events are sure to have a severe economic impact on the world.

With the sounding of the second trumpet, God will have issued His second divine warning designed to bring about repentance.

Trumpet Three (Rev. 8:10–11)

John looked and listened as a third angel sounded his trumpet. Immediately, *"a great star, blazing like a torch, fell from the sky on a third of the rivers, and on the springs of water"* (Rev. 8:10). This time, the blast was aimed at the earth's fresh water supply. In an instant, one-third of the earth's fresh water supply, desperately needed by humanity to survive, was contaminated and made bitter. The result was that many of the people who drank the bitter water died (Rev. 8:11).

Once again, John was not given many of the details concerning the means by which God would bring about the destruction. He is told that the star that fell upon the springs was named "Wormwood" (Rev. 8:11). In that day, wormwood was an extra bitter plant, which was usually not poisonous. However, in this particular case it must have been because John was told that many who drank the bitter water died.

Losing one-third of the earth's fresh water supply would severely cripple humanity's ability to survive for any length of time. However, the impact would not be limited to humans. The earth's animal population would also be affected by such a disaster. Also, farmers would find it difficult to acquire fresh water to irrigate their crops. All of these things would inevitably lead to a massive food shortage.

John watched as one by one, the elements of the earth's ecosystem were being systematically dismantled. It was as if God were unraveling the earth like a cat playing with a ball of yarn. Survival would become more and more difficult with each passing trumpet.

Once again, since the devastation was limited in its scope, the inhabitants of the earth were allowed a little more time to repent and come to Christ. We are not told how many took advantage of this opportunity.

Trumpet Four (Rev. 8:12)

With the first three trumpets having doled out their devastation on the dry land, sea, and fresh waters respectively, John's attention was turned to the destruction that was soon to be poured out on the earth's atmosphere through the fourth trumpet. As the fourth trumpet was sounded, John reported that *"a third of the sun was struck, a third of the moon, and a third of the stars, so that a third of them turned dark"* (Rev. 8:12). John also wrote that *"a third of the day was without light, and also a third of the night"* (Rev. 8:12).

The sun, moon, and stars that God had spoken into existence on the fourth day of creation were now being darkened by God. The statement that one-third of each were struck and turned dark could mean one of two things. Either their output was dimmed by one-third, or they went completely dark for one-third of the time they would normally have shone on the earth. Taking into account what Jesus had shared with His disciples, it would seem that the second option is more accurate. Jesus told His disciples that the days would be cut short for the sake of the elect (Mt. 24:22). A literal interpretation would also seem to indicate that eight of the twenty-four hours of each day were completely without light.

A reduction of sunlight upon the earth by 33 percent would have a devastating effect on the world. Crops would not have the right amount of sunlight needed to properly develop. The temperature of the earth's atmosphere would also be dramatically lowered. The delicate balance that God has maintained since the creation of the earth would be upset as He poured out His judgment on the earth and sky.

Because all the different environmental systems of the earth are interconnected, it is highly probable that each of the first four trumpets will closely follow the one before it. It will seem like a long string of dominos that falls one by one until they are all lying flat. Once again, the devastation is severe, but it is limited in its scope, allowing time for the inhabitants of the earth to repent and turn to God. Soon it will be too late!

CHAPTER FIFTEEN
SMART BOMBS

The first four trumpets must have been pretty intense for John to witness. With the sound of the fourth trumpet still echoing in John's ear, God sent an eagle across the sky with a message for the remaining inhabitants of the earth. This provided a brief interlude for John to catch his breath and prepare himself for what remained to be revealed.

Most would agree that this eagle is not to be understood as a literal eagle, since literal eagles do not possess a human voice. Of course, Balaam might have said the same thing about donkeys before God spoke to him through his four-legged beast (Numbers 22). Either way, the inhabitants of the earth are warned by God that more devastation lies just around the corner.

The eagle's warnings are directed to the "inhabitants of the earth" (Rev. 8:13), most likely a reference to those who were still not prepared to meet God. As we have seen earlier, those who belong to God have been sealed and protected from the coming wrath of God (Rev. 7:3). In fact, during the sixth trumpet, mention is made specifically of this protection offered by God (Rev. 9:4).

Those who have surrendered their lives to God and have been sealed by Him are not going to be the objects of God's wrath. Jesus took the wrath they deserved upon Himself when He died upon the cross of Calvary (see Jn. 3:36; Rom. 1:18, 5:9; 1 Thess. 5:9). While believers will not be removed from the earth during this time, they will be protected by the hand of God. This will be done in much the same way that God protected the Israelites while executing His judgment upon Pharaoh and the Egyptians. This same type of protection was offered to Noah and his family members as God carried them through the flood, while the rest of humanity was swept away.

The eagle issues three "woes," which serve as warnings of the pending judgment. These three woes are linked to the next three trumpets that are about to be sounded. The first woe follows the fifth trumpet (Rev. 9:12). The second woe follows the sixth trumpet (Rev. 11:14). And, the final woe is promised immediately after that (Rev. 11:14).

Once again, the reader of Scripture can see how patient and longsuffering God is toward those that He has created. He offers repeated warnings for mankind to turn to Him before it is too late. Like a man on the side of the road holding up a sign warning passers-by of a washed-out bridge, God holds up one sign after another warning the inhabitants of the earth that danger lies ahead for all who do not heed His warnings. While some will heed His warnings and turn their lives around, others will keep the pedal to the metal and plunge headfirst into an eternity without God.

With each of the eagle's three warnings the suspense builds, the tempo increases, and the destruction shifts from affecting the atmospheric elements to directly affecting humanity. During the next two trumpets, John is provided with more details than in the previous four. This again follows the rhythmic pattern set forth in the seal visions.

Trumpet Five (Rev. 9:1–12)

In this expanded scene, John is permitted to see a star that has fallen from the sky to the earth. He is not told who the star represents, but in most biblical literature a star that has fallen from the sky to the earth symbolizes an evil spirit or demonic angel. What makes this star important is that he has been given the key to the shaft of the Abyss so that he might open it and allow the perpetrators of the next trumpet to come forth and execute God's wrath on those who have not been sealed with God's mark. With the precision of a modern-day smart bomb, God will target those who do not have a relationship with Him.

The term Abyss literally means "the place without depth." The "bottomless pit" is the way some translations describe it. John's contemporaries viewed the universe much like a three-story building. The basement was symbolic of the underworld (the Abyss, Hell, etc.). The first floor would be the earth upon which they lived. And, the top floor represented the heavens where God dwelt.

The Abyss is pictured as the dwelling place of the demonic locusts with scorpion-like stingers. God allowed them to be released from the Abyss so that they could inflict painful torture upon all who had rejected Him. They were not given free reign to do as they pleased, but instead they had to operate under the restraints that God had established. Again, God remains in complete control throughout this entire time of tribulation.

John informed his readers of the limits that God placed on the demonic locusts. He wrote: *"They were told not to harm the grass of the earth or any plant or tree, but only those people who did not have the seal of God on their foreheads. They were not given power to kill them, but only to torture them for five months"* (Rev. 9:4–5). John's readers knew the terrible damage that a swarm of locusts would inflict on the grass, plants, and trees of any land they invaded. A swarm of locusts would literally strip the land bare, leaving nothing in its wake. Joel offers a detailed description of the devastation left behind following a locust plague (see the book of Joel).

Normal locusts do not attack humans, but John was informed that these locusts were different. They were not sent to harm the land. They were sent to torture those who had rejected God's gracious offer of forgiveness (Rev. 9:4). Their scorpion-like tails released a nonfatal poison that inflicted an enormous amount of pain upon the recipients of their stings.

Once again, God's people were spared the brunt of the end-time judgment as the locusts were forbidden from harming those who had been marked by God (Rev. 9:4). Those without the mark of God were not so blessed.

The locusts were sent to inflict painful torture upon the inhabitants of the earth who lacked God's divine mark. The torture was to last five months. It is not known if this is to be understood as a literal five months or simply a limited amount of time. The normal life span of a locust was typically five months (from springtime through the summer months), so God may have simply been implying that for a short season the torture would continue. Either way, God limited the length of time the torture would last. This is, once again, a sign of His mercy toward those who have repeatedly rejected His offer of forgiveness.

The irony of the whole scene is that the demonic locusts, who operate as servants of Satan, inflict so much pain on their earthly counterparts that those being tortured would *"seek death, but will not find it; they will long to die, but death will elude them"* (Rev. 9:6). This is further evidence that evil has no bounds—it will even destroy its own if given the opportunity.

John leaned in to take a closer look at the swarm of demonic locusts. Through his description, his readers are given a glimpse into the demonic world through the use of his figurative language and symbols (Rev. 9:7–11). While no one can know for certain all that is communicated through these symbols, several things stand out. First, they were well-trained and well-prepared as *"horses prepared for battle."* Next, John reported that they *"wore something like crowns of gold"* symbolizing their futile attempt to appear powerful and important. In a couple of ways they resembled humans (a man's face, a woman's hair). Their bite was described as that of a lion. They were protected by a breastplate of iron. The sound of their wings was reminiscent of powerful armies that thundered down the road on their way into battle. While they did not possess the power to take human life, they did possess the power to torment humans to the point that humans wished they were dead.

As John looked to the front of the line, he was given a glimpse of their leader. He reported that their "king" was the "angel of the Abyss," whose name meant "destroyer" (Rev. 9:11). It is unclear exactly who this might be, but most will rule out Satan because he has yet to be bound and cast into the Abyss. It is probably some high-ranking demon placed in charge of the other demons.

With the closing of this scene, John let his readers know the first woe had passed, but the other two were coming soon.

Trumpet Six (Rev. 9:13–21)

No sooner had the curtain closed on the previous scene than it reopened to reveal the sixth trumpet. John must have felt overwhelmed with the magnitude of all that he was witnessing. Even though the demonic locusts of the last scene were not permitted to claim the lives of their victims, that was about to change during this next trumpet.

John heard a voice coming from the horns of the altar of incense. This was the same altar under which he had seen the souls of the martyrs (Rev. 6:9–11) and upon which he had seen the incense mixed with the prayers of the saints (Rev. 8:3–5). From that altar, a voice commanded the angel with the sixth trumpet to release the four demonic angels who had been bound at the great river Euphrates (Rev. 9:14). This river was viewed as the ancient boundary marker between the nation of Israel and its enemies. This scene revealed that the enemies of mankind had been restrained at the borders, waiting for God to release them to inflict their destruction on mankind.

These four angels are said to have remained bound at this location, *"ready for this very hour and day and month and year"* (Rev. 9:15). This terminology was used to stress the sovereignty of God who had planned out every detail of His exit strategy. The fact that God could keep these harmful angels bound until He was ready to release them demonstrates that they are subject to Him in every way.

John looked on as they were released by God to carry out their grim mission across the face of the earth. Their mission was to kill one-third of mankind (Rev. 9:15). Whereas, Christians were protected during the fifth trumpet, no mention is made of that type of protection during the sixth trumpet. In fact, those who were forced to endure the torture of the previous trumpet will probably want to get revenge on those who were exempt from the pain.

Already, one-fourth of the world's population had been destroyed by the sword during the fourth seal, and now a third of those who remained were going to being killed. To put that number in perspective let's do the math. Suppose the world's population at the beginning of the tribulation was near what it is today—around six billion people. If that were the case, then 1.5 billion people would have died during the fourth seal, leaving 4.5 billion on the earth. If another third of that number were wiped out, that would add another 1.5 billion to the list of those killed in a short amount of time (a total of 3 billion dead). This number would not include the many people who died in the ships that were destroyed during the second trumpet, or the many Christians who were martyred because of their faith in Christ. This would mean that less than half of those who began the tribulation period would make it past the sixth trumpet.

As you can see, the intensity of these events continue to increase with each passing judgment, just as the pains of childbirth increase in intensity as a woman nears the birth of her child. You will surely remember that this was noted on Jesus' map of the end-times (Mt. 24:8).

As in the previous trumpet, the enemy of mankind was demonic, not human. The leaders of this massive army are the evil angels that had been bound, but were now released. They gathered their demonic comrades and rode off into battle. John was told that the number of their mounted troops was two hundred million (Rev. 9:16). It matters very little to John's message whether this number was meant to be taken literally or symbolically. The army that would be used to claim the lives of one-third of humanity would be immune to the bullets and bombs of any nation's army. Therefore, no nation would be exempt from their destruction.

In Revelation 9:17–19, John describes the horses and their riders in vivid terms. Many suggest that his description is reminiscent of the most feared army of that day—the Parthians—whose archers were well known for their ability to strike their enemies dead by shooting forward and to the rear. In other words, they were very skilled and accurate. While it is obvious this was not the army being described in this text, by describing the demonic army in this way, John's audience would have understood the strength of the demonic foe that will ride forth in that day.

Much to John's amazement, *"The rest of mankind that were not killed by these plagues still did not repent of the works of their hands; they did not stop worshiping demons, and idols of gold, silver, bronze, stone and wood—idols that cannot see or hear or walk."* (Rev. 9:20). Instead, of worshiping the One who could save them, they worshiped the idols their hands had created. This was another example of the grip that idolatry will have on those who practice it. As sunlight melts wax but hardens clay, so the events of the end will soften the hearts of those who turn to God while hardening the hearts of those who resist God's offer of grace and forgiveness. In so doing, the true nature of their hearts will be revealed for all to see.

These survivors also refused to turn away from their lives of murder, sorcery, sexual immorality, and theft (Rev. 9:21). Their lives were totally consumed with self-indulgence. Their response to God's graciousness lines up perfectly with what the other New Testament writers predicted would occur in the final days (2 Tim. 3:1–5, 4:3–4).

CHAPTER SIXTEEN

THE BITTERSWEET TASTE OF WAR

Following the sixth trumpet another interlude is included before the sounding of the seventh trumpet. This was also a part of the rhythmic pattern that had begun with the seals. Again, the reader must remember these interludes serve several purposes. First, they demonstrate the distinct differences that exist between those who belong to God and those who do not. They also provide additional information that helps the rest of the drama make more sense. And finally, they remind those facing persecution that God is implementing His exit strategy in the midst of their suffering, and as a result, they can live each day with the confidence that He is in control.

This is quite a lengthy interlude that is composed of several parts, which must be interpreted as a whole. In other words, one part does not make sense without the other parts. To split up a passage that John intended to be understood as a whole will only lead to a misinterpretation of the passage.

Thunders Sealed, Mystery Accomplished (Rev. 10:1–7)

A beautiful picture was painted for John of an angel descending from Heaven holding a small scroll in his hand. As he descended, he let out a loud shout to which "seven thunders" responded with a revelation that must have been grand to experience. As John had grown accustomed to doing, he began recording what the "thunders" had spoken. This time, however, a voice from Heaven instructed him, *"Seal up what the seven thunders have said and do not write it down"* (Rev. 10:4). Because John obeyed the voice from Heaven, no one knows what was communicated to him. Little is gained by spending time speculating on the content of those "seven thunders." Had God wanted us to have that information, He would not have ordered John to seal it up.

Since John obeyed God and omitted that information from his written account, we can know for certain that there are some things concerning the end we will have to wait to learn. This reinforces the truth that the book of Revelation was not given to answer all of our questions. While God has revealed all we need to know to prepare ourselves for the end, He is not obligated to answer every inquiry we make. There are some things that He has chosen to seal until the end.

As the interlude unfolds before John, the mighty angel swears an oath using God's name. John recorded his promise with these words: *"There will be no more delay! But in the day when the seventh angel is about to sound his trumpet, the mystery of God will be accomplished, just as he announced to his servants the prophets"* (Rev. 10:6–7). The angel was warning that with the blowing of the seventh trumpet the mystery of God would be accomplished (completed, finished).

What was this mystery of which he was speaking? Paul explained the mystery in Ephesians 3:2–6. Notice the similar terminology:

> *Surely you have heard about the administration of God's grace that was given to me for you, that is, the mystery made known to me by revelation, as I have already written briefly. In reading this, then, you will be able to understand my insight into the mystery of Christ, which was not made known to men in other generations as it has now been revealed by the Spirit to God's holy apostles and prophets. This mystery is that through the gospel the Gentiles are heirs together with Israel, members together of one body, and sharers together in the promise in Christ Jesus.*

The mystery that had been made known to the apostles and prophets will be brought to completion at this point in history. The mystery about which John spoke was that through the gospel, the Jews and Gentiles have been made one in Christ. God has been forming one family out of the two groups, and with the blowing of the seventh trumpet the family will be complete. Three times in this brief text Paul links the two groups together using the three complementary phrases, "heirs together," "members together," and "sharers together."

Just as He had done in the previous interlude between the sixth seal and the seventh seal, God emphasized the unity of the two groups. This message is repeated again and again throughout the New Testament.

> *Therefore, remember that formerly you who are Gentiles by birth and called "uncircumcised" by those who call themselves "the circumcision" (that done in the body by the hands of men)—remember that at that time you were separate from Christ, excluded from citizenship in Israel and foreigners to the covenants of the promise, without hope and without God in the world. But now in Christ Jesus you who once were far away have been brought near through the blood of Christ. For he himself is our peace, who has made the two one and has destroyed the barrier, the dividing wall of hostility, by abolishing in his flesh the law with its commandments and regulations. His purpose was to create in himself one new man out of the two, thus making peace, and in this one body to reconcile both of them to God through the cross, by which he put to death their hostility. He came and preached peace to you who were far away and peace to those who were near. For through him we both have access to the Father by one Spirit* (Eph. 2:11–18).

Those who had been excluded in the past were now included in Christ, fulfilling God's purpose of creating one out of the two. Both groups have been reconciled to God through the cross of Christ. In another letter, Paul wrote:

> *You are all sons of God through faith in Christ Jesus, for all of you who were baptized into Christ have clothed yourselves with Christ. There is neither Jew nor Greek, slave nor free, male nor female, for you are all one in Christ Jesus. If you belong to Christ, then you are Abraham's seed, and heirs according to the promise* (Gal. 3:26–29).

The dispensationalists who insist on keeping these two groups separate are in clear violation of the explicit teaching of God's Word. This error causes them to miss the meaning of the interlude under consideration.

Through His angel, God was also warning that the eternal family, which He was forming, was soon to be complete. The day was coming when the last member would be grafted into the family tree, and no more names would be added to the Lamb's Book of Life. In this interlude, the angel explained the timing of the last addition. He stated that the mystery would be accomplished (the final addition made) *"in the days when the seventh angel is about to sound his trumpet"* (Rev. 10:7). Did you catch what John just said? The completion of the eternal family will coincide with the sounding of the seventh trumpet.

Don't miss this critically important piece of information. John is stating that after the blowing of the seventh trumpet, which will mark the return of Christ, no other souls would be saved. No one else would be added to the family of God. This is huge! This forces us to reevaluate our interpretation of all the other events that will follow the seventh trumpet. It means that no one will come to Christ during the seven bowls of wrath, or the thousand-year reign.

If my understanding is correct, the eternal destiny of all mankind will be sealed at this point in time. I realize that many would disagree with me, but I see no other way to correctly interpret John's message. To further support this claim, one cannot find in Scripture any mention of anyone else coming to Christ after the blowing of the seventh trumpet. All that remains is for the wrath of God to be poured out on those who have rejected His offer of salvation.

Jesus Himself often taught that the day was coming when it would no longer be possible for a person to come to Him. Remember the three parables of Christ concerning the ten bridesmaids, the three servants, and the sheep and the goats? In each of these parables, Jesus made it clear that no further opportunities would be offered after His return. If Christ's return coincides with the blowing of the seventh trumpet, it would seem that all the pieces of the puzzle fit together perfectly. But wait . . . it seems we are getting ahead of ourselves.

Bittersweet Message (Rev. 10:8–11:4)

Next, John was invited to become a participant in the divine drama much like an historian who is embedded with a military unit. As he stepped forward, he was told to take the scroll that was in the hand of the mighty angel and eat it. As he took it, he was warned that it would be sweet in his mouth, and then turn sour in his stomach. Of course, the text is not insinuating that John actually ate a literal scroll, but rather that he internalized the message contained in the scroll.

Sure enough, just as he had been warned, the content of the scroll was bittersweet. The message started out sweet as honey, but it soon turned into something sour. He was then told that he *"must prophesy again about many peoples, nations, languages and kings"* (Rev. 10:11). In contrast to the message of the seven thunders, which he was commanded to seal up, this was a message he was to openly share.

In a scene that sounds bizarre today, John is told to take a measuring rod and measure the temple of God, to count its worshipers, but to exclude the outer court of the Gentiles (Rev. 11:1–2). There has been much debate over why God would tell John to do this. Some suggest it was because the temple was about to be destroyed, and John would need to know the temple's dimensions in order for it to be rebuilt later. Those who hold this view point to the occasions in the Old Testament where the prophets or priests were told to measure Jerusalem before it was destroyed so it could be rebuilt when they returned from exile. If that were the reason in this particular case, one would think that John would have recorded the measurements. He did not.

Others claim that John was told to measure the temple as a statement that God was going to spare it from the destruction that was coming upon Jerusalem. In that case, the measurements would seem unnecessary since the building would still be standing for all to see.

What *does* make sense is that God was not speaking of a literal temple, but of His followers whom the New Testament refers to as the "temple of the Holy Spirit" (1 Cor. 3:16–17). In much the same way as the 144,000 were marked in the first interlude, so John was to measure (or make note of) those who make up the "temple" of God. It was not that God did not know who belonged to Him; He certainly did. The exercise

John was participating in was not for God's benefit, it was for the benefit of His followers. God told John to identify His followers because they were about to be the subjects of what John was to be shown next.

This also explains why John was told to only count the worshipers in the inner court, and not those in the outer court. In the Jewish temple, non-Jews were only allowed to enter into the outer court—no farther. If they went beyond that point, they risked being executed. At least when it came to the temple, it was very clear who were Jews and who were not. God was about to make just as clear of a distinction between those who belonged to Him and those who did not.

John was also told that the outer court would be given to the Gentiles (a reference to non-Christians), and they would trample on the holy city for forty-two months (Rev. 11:2). Again, interpreting this passage in its context will not allow for a literal "temple," "outer court," or "holy city." These are all Jewish word pictures used to communicate God's central message. Since Christ called His followers *"a city set on a hill that cannot be hidden"* (Mt. 5:14), this reference to the Gentiles trampling the holy city is best understood to mean that non-Christians will not respond favorably toward those who are Christians. They will persecute, or trample upon, those who are genuine followers of Christ.

Here is where things get a little more difficult to understand. John reported that the opposition the Christians will face will last for forty-two months. He also stated that God's witnesses will prophesy for 1260 days. It is clear that 42 months is the same as 1260 days (or 3 ½ years). While that much is clear, it is not clear exactly how John meant for that time period to be understood. The imagery he used stemmed from a passage in Daniel 12 where the prophet asked how long it would be before the prophecy he was being shown would be fulfilled (Dan. 12:6). The angel responded to Daniel by saying, "It will be for a time, times, and half a time" (Dan. 12:7). This phrase literally meant three and a half "times" (1 + 2 + ½ = 3 ½ "times"). In the context in which Daniel wrote, it was understood to simply mean a limited time of great suffering.

It is for this reason many will suggest this phrase, and similar phrases that John used throughout the book of Revelation, was not meant to be interpreted literally. Instead they were meant to be understood as figures of speech representing a limited time of great suffering. By using this idiom, many of John's readers would have instantly understood what John had in mind.

Perhaps those who see these phrases as representing a limited, but unspecified time of great suffering are correct. I cannot say for certain, but one thing is for sure, John uses many different variations of this phrase throughout the rest of the book of Revelation. He mentions 3 ½ years, 3 ½ days, 42 months, 1260 days, and "time, times, and half a time." All are used somewhat interchangeably in the telling of his prophecy.

Perhaps we can still glean the main message of John's story without having to know for certain the exact timetable he had in mind. First, we know that the persecution the Christians will endure as the result of their proclamation will last the entire time that they prophesy. Their persecution will last 42 months and their proclamation will last 1260 days—the exact same length of time. So, John's message to Christians was that as long as they proclaim God's message, the lost world will oppose them. That much we know to be true!

Next, John told us about the "witnesses" that would proclaim God's gospel to the lost world. He likens their character and their work to four Old Testament heroes: Moses, Elijah, Zerubbabel, and Joshua. Notice how John compares the witnesses to these four men. He refers to them as the two olive trees and the two lamp stands that are in the presence of the Lord (Rev. 11:4). This description links the witnesses to Joshua, an Old Testament high priest, and Zerubbabel, an Old Testament governor, or king. Both of these men were likened to olive trees next to a lamp stand in the Old Testament book of Zechariah (Zech. 3–4). He also compared the character and the work of the "witnesses" to Elijah, the great Old Testament prophet, by stating that *"they will have power to shut up the sky so that it will not rain during the time they are prophesying"* (Rev. 11:6). He also likened them to Moses, the great ambassador of deliverance, when he referenced the power they possessed to turn water into blood and to strike the earth with every kind of plague as often as they want (Rev. 11:6).

In providing these descriptions, John was not claiming that these four Old Testament heroes would be brought back to life. He was not stating that these four men would become super-evangelists who would win the world to Christ on their own. After all, he only referred to two witnesses, not four. Instead, John was describing the character of those who would carry out God's mission on earth. He was simply stating that these witnesses would be similar to Joshua, Zerubbabel, Elijah, and Moses.

If this is true, then we need to ask in what ways the witnesses would be like these four men. The answer is really quite simple. God's witnesses would be prophets, priests, kings, and ambassadors in the Lord's service. These are all responsibilities that have been assigned to every follower of Christ, not to just two individuals who will work alone in the final days.

I believe that the tale of the two witnesses is a story of the Church's work in the midst of persecution. This story is not the tale of two individuals who single-handedly work to share the gospel of Christ in the final days. That responsibility (sharing the gospel) has been committed to every follower of Christ by the Savior Himself—not to just two individuals. It was Jesus Himself who commissioned all of His followers to be His witnesses throughout the world. He explained that responsibility (and privilege) when He said, *"YOU WILL RECEIVE POWER when the Holy Spirit comes on you; and YOU WILL BE MY WITNESSES in Jerusalem, and in all Judea and Samaria, and to the ends of the earth"* (Acts 1:8, emphasis added).

Jesus' commission has not expired, but instead, it has been passed on from one generation of believers to the next. All true followers of Christ have been empowered by the Holy Spirit and are responsible to carry the gospel to the ends of the earth. This has never been the responsibility of just one or two "supernaturally gifted" people. Nor, will it ever be!

For this reason, it is best to understand the "two witnesses," not as two individuals, but as the body of Christ. If this is the case, why would John list two witnesses and not just one? Again, the context will provide us with the answer to that question.

This entire interlude is about God's family, which is comprised of two groups (Jews and Gentiles) that have been made one in Christ. Perhaps it was God's way of demonstrating how the Jews and Gentiles will work together in those final days to take the gospel to the world. As the rest of this interlude will demonstrate, they will not only work together to fulfill

God's mission, but they will suffer together, they will die together, and they will be raised to eternal life together. Perhaps it is for this reason that God uses two witnesses in this story.

What John was observing was the enactment of the bittersweet message contained in the scroll he had just finished eating. It was sweet to know that God would protect His witnesses while they shared His message. But, it was bitter to see that they would be attacked, overpowered, killed, and left exposed in the streets while their enemies celebrated their defeat. The last part of the message was perhaps the sweetest part of all: they would be resurrected and taken to Heaven in the presence of those who had killed them. The victory celebration would be incredible.

Like the first interlude, this interlude offered hope to the whole family of God. Now that we understand the participants in the drama, let's take a deeper look at what God says about their work.

According to John's account, the two witnesses were provided all the protection and power they needed to fulfill their God-given mission. Just as Jesus had promised to build His Church without allowing the forces of Hell to prevail against it (Mt. 16:18), here He confirms that promise. Jesus promised His followers they would possess supernatural power once the Holy Spirit was given to them at Pentecost (Acts 1:8, 2:1–4). Indwelt by the Holy Spirit, all true believers possess the power needed to fulfill their individual missions in this world. Satan is powerless to prevent them from succeeding.

John reported that God's witnesses were assigned the task of prophesying—proclaiming the good news of salvation to the world (Rev. 11:3). They would do so in the midst of great suffering (Rev. 11:2). Despite the persecution they would face, they would succeed in carrying out their mission. God will protect them and provide all that they need while they fulfill His mission for them. It is not until their work is done that Satan and his associates will be able to silence their voices. John wrote: *"When they finished their testimony, the beast that comes up from the Abyss will attack them, and overpower and kill them"* (Rev. 11:7).

This interlude should be understood as a message of hope to all Christians. Satan will not be allowed to take the life of any Christian before God determines that their individual work on earth is complete. This is true for all Christians of all times, not just those living in the final days. Satan does not have the power to silence the voice of any believer before they have completed the work God has assigned to them. Satan has to work under the authority of God—under the limits and boundaries God has set. This wonderful knowledge allows Christians to be bold in their faith. Satan can only do what God allows, and only according to His timetable.

John explained that those who came against the witnesses would be devoured by "fire" that came from the mouths of the witnesses. He obviously did not mean for that to be taken literally, but instead was referring to the power of the words the witnesses would be speaking. The power to silence the ignorance of their enemies will come from the spoken Word of God, empowered by the Holy Spirit. In fact, later in the interlude he confirms that the message the witnesses proclaimed had "tormented those who live on earth" (Rev. 11:10).

Only after Christians have completed their individual missions, will Satan's forces be allowed to attack them, overpower them, and kill them. John was shown the contempt that the world will have for believers when he was told that the beast will refuse to bury the bodies of the dead saints. In John's day, it was a huge insult for a person's body to be refused a proper burial. Again, this imagery was not meant to be taken literally, but to show the contempt that Satan and his followers will have for God's children.

Not only will they show contempt toward God's people, but they will celebrate the killing of Christians. John wrote: *"For three and a half days men from every people, tribe, language and nation will gaze on their bodies and refuse them burial. The inhabitants of the earth will gloat over them and will celebrate by sending each other gifts, because these two prophets had tormented those who live on the earth"* (Rev. 11:9–10).

The message the Church is called to proclaim will torment the lost world to the point that they will celebrate as Christians are killed. John does not want to gloss over the contempt that the world will show toward Christians, but instead to place that contempt in its proper context. He wants Christians to know that Satan cannot stop the work of God. He cannot take a Christian's life prematurely. God is in complete control.

As difficult as those days will be, God reminds Christians that evil will not be allowed to triumph for long. John reported, *"After the three and a half days a breath of life from God entered them, and they stood on their feet, and terror struck those who saw them. Then they heard a loud voice from heaven saying to them, 'Come up here.' And they went up to heaven in a cloud, while their enemies looked on"* (Rev. 11:11–12).

This resurrection will occur as Christ returns for those who belong to Him. These are the same people John took note of at the beginning of the interlude—those who make up the temple of God that John was told to measure. They will be resurrected at the time of the "severe earthquake" while all of the onlookers (those who persecuted the Church) watch their resurrection and *"give glory to the God of heaven"* (Rev. 11:13).

Please understand that John was not saying these onlookers repented and were saved. He simply stated that they gave God the glory that was due Him. This is similar to what Paul said would occur at the end when he wrote: *"At the name of Jesus, every knee should bow . . . every tongue confess that Jesus is Lord to the glory of God the Father"* (Phil. 2:10–11). Paul certainly did not mean that all the inhabitants of the earth would be saved, and neither did John intend for that meaning to be implied to this passage. John was not describing an event that would occur prior to the second coming of Christ when men could still come to Christ. He was describing the resurrection that will occur as Christ breaks through the clouds and gathers all those who belong to Him (1 Thess. 4:13-18). At that point in time, it will be too late for anyone else to be saved; they will simply give glory to God.

Taken as a whole, this interlude warns believers of the bittersweet times that lie ahead. God, who is fully aware of all who belong to Him, will empower His followers to take His message to the ends of the earth, proclaiming it with great power and protection. Only after their mission is complete will they suffer death, but death will not have the final word. After a short time, God will resurrect them in the presence of those who have opposed them so they might spend their eternity with Him.

It is interesting to note that Paul's description of the rise of the man of lawlessness in the final days is very similar to John's description of the times in which the Church will carry on its work. It is some time during this point of the tribulation that the antichrist will proclaim himself to be God. That event is known as the Abomination of Desolation. Notice the similarities in John's account and Paul's account:

> *Concerning the coming of our Lord Jesus Christ and our being gathered to him, we ask you, brothers, not to become easily unsettled or alarmed by some prophecy, report or letter supposed to have come from us, saying that the day of the Lord has already come. Don't let anyone deceive you in any way, for that day will not come until the rebellion occurs and the man of lawlessness is revealed, the man doomed to destruction. He will oppose and will exalt himself over everything that is called God or is worshiped, so that he sets himself up in God's temple, proclaiming himself to be God. Don't you remember that when I was with you I used to tell you these things? And now you know what is holding him back, so that he may be revealed at the proper time. For the secret power of lawlessness is already at work; but the one who now holds it back will continue to do so till he is taken out of the way. And then the lawless one will be revealed, whom the Lord Jesus will overthrow with the breath of his mouth and destroy by the splendor of his coming. The coming of the lawless one will be in accordance with the work of Satan displayed in all kinds of counterfeit miracles, signs and wonders, and in every sort of evil that deceives those who are perishing. They perish because they refused to love the truth and so be saved. For this reason God sends them a powerful delusion so that they will believe the lie and so that all will be condemned who have not believed the truth but have delighted in wickedness* (2 Thess. 2:1–12).

Both accounts demonstrate God's sovereignty and control as He implements His grand plan. Both show that the enemy's power and influence are restrained by God. Both place the rise of the evil one prior to the rapture (resurrection of believers). Both illustrate the arrogance of the wicked. And, both demonstrate that God and His followers achieve the ultimate victory.

As Jesus warned His disciples about these days, He said that the distress of these days would be *"unequaled from the beginning of the world until now—and never to be equaled again*" (Mt. 24:21). While the days of distress will be dark days for believers, they will not last forever. John is told that after three and a half days (a relatively short period of time) those who have endured the attacks of the evil one would be resurrected and raptured before the eyes of their enemies. In other words, God will not let Satan gloat for long. About the time that Satan lights up his celebration cigar, God will step in and claim the ultimate victory.

With this interlude complete, John is further prepared for the wonderful message contained in the seventh and final trumpet—the trumpet of victory!

CHAPTER SEVENTEEN

EXTRACTING THE GROUND FORCES

As we prepare to examine the seventh trumpet, it will be important to remember the word picture I shared with you earlier. I compared the seventh trumpet to a hospital room with a curtain dividing it in half. One side of the room was bright and the other side was dark. The bright side had a window with the blinds temporarily closed, and the dark side had seven exhibits where the seven bowls of God's wrath were individually displayed.

Before viewing the seven exhibits on the dark side of the room, John's attention is first drawn toward the sound of joyful voices, which seem to be coming from outside the window in that room. John walks over to take a closer look. There, he learns what the seventh trumpet is all about.

Trumpet Seven: (Rev. 11:15–19)

Unlike the seventh seal, which began with silence throughout Heaven, the blowing of the seventh trumpet brought forth loud voices from Heaven, which proclaimed the end of the *"kingdom of the world"* and the beginning of the *"kingdom of our Lord and of his Christ"* (Rev. 11:15). The voices proclaimed that His reign had begun, and that it would continue "forever and ever" (Rev. 11:15).

The reason these proclamations are resounding throughout Heaven is that the time has come for God's children to finally be home with their Savior. As John will soon be shown (Rev. 14:14–20), the rapture of the Church is linked to the blowing of the seventh trumpet. Thus, when John heard that final trumpet, he also heard the multitudes in Heaven proclaiming, *"The time has come for judging the dead, and for rewarding your servants the prophets and your saints and those who reverence your name both great and small—and for destroying those who destroy the earth"* (Rev. 11:18).

The timing of this event should be no surprise to students of the Bible. Over and over again, Scripture links the return of Christ to this final trumpet. Jesus predicted such when He said:

> *Immediately after the distress of those days "the sun will be darkened, and the moon will not give its light; the stars will fall from the sky, and the heavenly bodies will be shaken." At that time the sign of the Son of Man will appear in the sky, and all the nations of the earth will mourn. They will see the Son of Man coming on the clouds of the sky, with power and great glory. And he will send his angels with a loud trumpet call, and they will gather his elect from the four winds, from one end of the heavens to the other* (Mt. 24:29–31).

Paul said the same thing when he wrote:

> *Listen, I tell you a mystery: We will not all sleep, but we will all be changed—in a flash, in the twinkling of an eye, at the last trumpet. For the trumpet will sound, the dead will be raised imperishable, and we will be changed. For the perishable must clothe itself with the imperishable, and the mortal with immortality. When the perishable has been clothed with the imperishable, and the mortal with immortality, then the saying that is written will come true: "Death has been swallowed up in victory." "Where, O death, is your victory? Where, O death, is your sting?"* (1 Cor. 15:51–55).

And yet, in another place Paul stated:

> *Brothers, we do not want you to be ignorant about those who fall asleep, or to grieve like the rest of men, who have no hope. We believe that Jesus died and rose again and so we believe that God will bring with Jesus those who have fallen asleep in him. According to the Lord's own word, we tell you that we who are still alive, who are left till the coming of the*

> *Lord, will certainly not precede those who have fallen asleep. For the Lord himself will come down from heaven, with a loud command, with the voice of the archangel and with the trumpet call of God, and the dead in Christ will rise first. After that, we who are still alive and are left will be caught up together with them in the clouds to meet the Lord in the air. And so, we will be with the Lord forever* (1 Thess. 4:13–17).

And finally, it was God's own angel who promised on oath that the trumpet would mark this glorious day. John recorded his promise with these words:

> *Then the angel I had seen standing on the sea and on the land raised his right hand to heaven. And he swore by him who lives for ever and ever, who created the heavens and all that is in them, the earth and all that is in it, and the sea and all that is in it, and said, "There will be no more delay! But in the days when the seventh angel is about to sound his trumpet, the mystery of God will be accomplished, just as he announced to his servants the prophets"* (Rev. 10:5–7).

As John was allowed a sneak peek through a crack in the blinds, he saw the twenty-four elders fully engaged in the worship of God. They had fallen on their faces in worship of God because He had asserted His great power and *"begun to reign"* (Rev. 11:17). They celebrated the rapture of God's own and the fact that His wrath was about to be poured out on the angry nations. As they worshiped, they anticipated the judging of the dead and the rewarding of the saved (Rev. 11:18).

Then, John was granted a brief glimpse into the temple in Heaven. As he looked into the temple he saw the Ark of the Covenant, which symbolized the presence of God during the Old Testament time period. This is the same temple out of which the seven angels holding the seven bowls of God's wrath will walk as the transition is made to the bowl judgments. By mentioning the temple, both now and again right before the introduction of the seven bowls of God's wrath (Rev. 15), he will connect the two series.

Before showing John the two harvest scenes that depict the rapture of God's children and the destruction of the unsaved, John was shown why such a distinction was needed between the two groups. In short, God answers the questions that must have been racing through John's mind: "How did things get this bad?" and "Where did things go so wrong?" God is about to answer those questions before he shows John a scene depicting the day for which all believers long—the rapture!

SECTION FIVE

FLASHBACK!

Chapters twelve through fourteen of Revelation provide some very valuable and much-needed information for John and his readers concerning how the world got in such a mess. While some claim that these chapters seem out of place, in reality, they are woven perfectly into the storyline. As a master storyteller, God strategically inserted these acts into His divine drama.

Chapters twelve, thirteen, and fourteen must be understood as a single unit composed of multiple parts. These three chapters provide justification for the incredible wrath that is about to be poured out in chapters fifteen and sixteen. Notice how this all fits together.

Following the announcement that the end has come—God's reign has begun, the faithful saints are about to be rewarded, and the enemies of God are about to be destroyed (chapter eleven)—chapter twelve explains why things were coming to such a violent end. The drama recorded here provides many details concerning the ongoing war that Satan has chosen to wage against God and His followers.

Chapter thirteen paints a picture of the wicked, "satanic trinity" that will work till the very end to carry out Satan's mission. Satan is the master of counterfeit. Each thing God creates, Satan offers a cheap imitation to entice people away from God. This chapter in the Bible shows his ultimate attempt to counterfeit God's Trinity.

Chapter fourteen is both a chapter of hope for those who have faithfully followed God, and a chapter of warning for those who have refused to make such a decision.

Through this portion of the drama, God offered John justification for what He was about to do to the enemies of God. It was not that God was required to justify any of His actions, but by providing this information He helped John understand the reason these things would occur. Through this interlude, God sets the stage for the rapture, which will be described using the image of a grain harvest, and the seven bowls of God's wrath, which will be described using the image of a grape harvest. In that regard, the timing of this interlude could not have been better. Let's take a look at each of its sections.

CHAPTER EIGHTEEN

PSY-OPS: "GETTING INSIDE THE ENEMY'S HEAD"

(REVELATION 12)

The drama of Revelation chapter twelve begins with the introduction of a red dragon who is positioning himself to kill a child that is about to be born to a woman. The woman gave birth to a son, and despite the dragon's best efforts, the son was not devoured; but instead, he was snatched up into Heaven to be with God. The woman fled to a place prepared for her by God, and, until her mission was complete (1260 days), she was cared for by God.

The descriptive language used throughout this scene helps us to identify the characters. The woman is described as being *"clothed with the sun, with the moon under her feet, and a crown of twelve stars on her head"* (Rev 12:1). She is heard crying out in pain as she prepared to give birth to a child (Rev. 12:2). John is later told that the child she bore was a son, who was to rule the nations with an iron scepter (Rev. 12:5). While some choose to identify the woman as Mary (mother of Jesus), other details supplied later would indicate that this was not what John had in mind. Instead, it is better to understand the woman as representing the true followers of God from within the Jewish nation through whom the Messiah (the son) came. In other words, the woman represents a group of people—the faithful Jews—and not just one person.

The great red dragon is described with colorful language as well. He is pictured as having seven heads and ten horns and seven crowns on his heads (Rev. 12:3). John was shown that his tail had *"swept a third of the stars out of the sky and flung them to the earth"* (Rev. 12:4). Based upon John's description, most would not deny that the great red dragon represents Satan, while the stars represent the fallen angels who were expelled out of Heaven along with him (Rev. 12:4). This expulsion from Heaven is described a few verses later (Rev. 12:7–9). Satan and his angels were clearly defeated as illustrated by them losing their place in Heaven and being hurled down to the earth. Satan is identified as, *"The great dragon . . . that ancient serpent, called the devil, or Satan, who leads the whole world astray"* (Rev. 12:9). In this battle, the strength of God's angelic army was shown superior to Satan and his fallen angels. Satan was *"hurled to earth, and his angels with him"* (Rev. 12:9).

Having lost their place in the heavenly realm, they sought to establish themselves as the rulers of the earthly realm. They set out to lead the whole world astray by usurping God's authority (Rev. 12:9). They attempted to put a stop to God's plan of redemption by killing His Son, Jesus. This is why John was shown the dragon standing *"in front of the woman who was about to give birth, so that he might devour her child the moment it was born"* (Rev. 12:4). Satan and his fallen angels must have thought that if they could kill Jesus, they would defeat Him. They were wrong. Jesus was not defeated when He was hung upon the cross, where he bled and died. Instead, He was victoriously resurrected by God and taken to Heaven where He remains to this day (Rev. 12:5).

Having failed to stop Jesus' work of redemption, the dragon went after His true followers. However, John was shown that despite the persecution and trials that the people of God would be required to endure (being sent to the "desert"), they would be protected, and provided for by God until their God-given mission (1260 days) was complete (Rev. 12:6). Doesn't that sound familiar to what we learned about the mission of the two witnesses?

To further illustrate this ultimate victory, a loud voice in Heaven was heard proclaiming the victory of Christ and His martyrs who followed Him all the way to death—loving Him more than they loved their own lives (Rev. 12:11). Even though, from an earthly perspective, it seemed that Satan had won the battle by snuffing out their lives, John was shown that from Heaven's perspective Satan had been bitterly defeated by the resurrection power of God.

As comforting as this would be to those who remained on the earth, the loud voice from Heaven warned them of Satan's fury, which would be directed at them *"because he knows that his time is short"* (Rev. 12:12). John was told that since Satan had lost his heavenly battle, he would re-direct all of his fury toward those who followed God. However, these followers would be divinely protected by God, out of the reach of Satan for "a time, times and half a time"—3 ½ years, or 1260 days (Rev. 12:14). In other words, Satan had no power to cut their God-given mission short. He was powerless to stop the work of God through them.

Despite Satan's greatest efforts, each generation of faithful Christ-followers will pass their faith on to the next generation of Christ-followers—their spiritual *"offspring"* (Rev. 12:17). As the initial generation of Christians completed the mission God had for them, Satan would direct his attacks at their offspring. John was told that Satan would wage war against *"the rest of her offspring—those who obey God's commands and hold to the testimony of Jesus"* (Rev. 12:17). This can be nothing other than a clear reference to the New Testament Church.

This passage provides further evidence that the Church is not immune from Satan's attacks, but neither does the Church have reason to be fearful of anything that Satan can do to it. While the Church will go through the difficult days of the end, God's providential plan will be accomplished no matter how hard Satan tries to thwart it. Even when it appears that Satan is winning the battle, one can rest assured that God has already won the war.

CHAPTER NINETEEN
AXIS OF EVIL

Chapter thirteen of Revelation provides us with a description of the leaders through whom Satan will work in the final days. Having been shown an overview of Satan's master plan, John is about to be shown the ones through whom Satan will seek to accomplish those goals. In this chapter, John is introduced to three "partners" who will do everything possible to lead people far from God. Similar to the Holy Trinity—God the Father, Son, and Holy Spirit—Satan will create his own "trinity." His "trinity" will be made up of the great red dragon (Satan himself), the beast out of the sea (commonly known as the antichrist), and the beast out of the earth (known as the false prophet). These three members will make up the satanic trinity. Their roles will mimic the roles of the real Trinity. The dragon (Satan) will try to usurp the role of God. The antichrist will claim to be Christ—the world's messiah. The false prophet will promise to guide the world into "truth," while leading them to believe his lies.

The things described in chapter thirteen will actually occur during the events mentioned in chapter twelve, not at some later time. This will be important to keep in mind.

The Beast Out of the Sea (Rev. 13:1-10)

A "beast" is introduced who has been commonly referred to as the "antichrist," although John never used that title for him. While he will be a "false-Christ" or "false-Messiah," John simply refers to him as the "beast." John is told that the beast came out of the "sea" (Rev. 13:1), a metaphor used in other places to describe the bottomless pit, or the Abyss (Rev. 11:7; 17:8).

This is later confirmed by John when he wrote: *"The beast, which you saw, once was, now is not, and will come up out of the Abyss and go to his destruction"* (Rev. 17:8).

The beast, or antichrist, is described for John using some pretty bizarre imagery that would later have to be explained to John (Rev. 13:1–2). For now, his characteristics were simply described so that John would be able to recognize him later on in the drama. Parts of the physical description of the beast match parts of the description given for the great red dragon of the previous chapter (Rev. 12:3). The beast will bear a great resemblance to Satan. Their connection is undeniable, for John is told, *"The dragon gave the beast his power and his throne and great authority"* (Rev. 13:2).

From John's account, it is clear that the beast will immerse himself in blasphemous schemes, which will be designed to intimidate followers of God. He will derive his power, his throne, and his authority from Satan (Rev. 13:2) whose work he will seek to carry out. Despite his greatest efforts, nothing he does will occur apart from the sovereign will of God. Everything Satan attempts to do will unknowingly play into the master plan that God has decreed will occur.

In some remarkable way, the beast will appear to have suffered a fatal head wound that has been miraculously healed. This "miracle mark" will create such a buzz that the lost world will willingly follow the beast (antichrist) and worship the dragon (Satan) who gave him his authority (Rev. 13:3–4). John recorded what his reign will be like.

> *The beast was given a mouth to utter proud words and blasphemies and to exercise his authority for forty-two months. He opened his mouth to blaspheme God, and to slander his name and his dwelling place and those who live in heaven. He was given power to make war against the saints and to conquer them. And he was given authority over every tribe, people, language and nation. All inhabitants of the earth will worship the beast—all whose names have not been written in the book of life belonging to the Lamb that was slain from the creation of the world* (Rev. 13:5–8).

As his popularity soars through the roof, he will begin to utter proud and blasphemous words against God, Heaven, and the inhabitants of Heaven (Rev. 13:5–6). He will be given power to make war against the saints and to eventually conquer them (Rev. 13:7). His rise to power and his reign of terror will be unlike anything the world has ever witnessed before. Christians will suffer greatly during this time. Many will die for refusing to denounce their faith in Christ. While the rest of the world will worship this beast, Christians will stand firm, even if it costs them their lives. Their boldness will serve as evidence of their genuine faith in Christ. While believers will suffer under the reign of the beast, they will rather die than to compromise their faith. They will become known for their *"patient endurance and faithfulness"* (Rev. 13:10).

Reading John's description of the beast's blasphemous words and his reign of terror, it is only natural to make the link between this event and the event known as the Abomination of Desolation that Jesus and Paul had promised. Remember that Paul promised that the rise of the beast (man of lawlessness) must occur before the second coming of Christ could take place (1 Thess. 2:1–4). This is just one other place the Bible confirms that the pretribulational view of the rapture cannot be accurate.

The Beast Out of the Earth (Rev. 13:11-18)

Next, John is introduced to a second beast that came out of the earth. He is later identified as the false prophet (Rev. 16:13, 19:20, 20:10). He is said to look like a lamb, but to speak like a dragon (Rev. 13:11). This is reminiscent of the description Jesus gave for the false prophets who outwardly appear to be sheep while on the inside they are actually ferocious wolves (Mt. 7:15). This beast clearly fits that description.

While the false prophet may claim to be divinely empowered and inspired, John makes it abundantly clear that his power and his message are not from God. His authority will be granted to him by the first beast (Rev. 13:12). In other words, he will operate with the antichrist's blessing because he will work to impose his agenda upon the inhabitants of the earth. This agenda will include forcing the inhabitants of the earth to worship the antichrist.

The false prophet will be granted the ability to perform great and miraculous signs, even causing fire to fall from Heaven to Earth (Rev. 13:13). The lost inhabitants of the earth will be deceived by the signs he performs. Jesus warned His followers about this day. You will remember His warning: *"If anyone says to you, 'Look, here is the Christ!' or, 'There he is!' do not believe it. For false prophets will appear and perform great signs and miracles to deceive even the elect—if that were possible"* (Mt. 24:23–24). In other words, Jesus was warning that the delusions of that day will be very hard to resist. Only true believers will see through the false prophet's lies.

The false prophet will even go as far as to set up an image of the beast, and then order that all people worship the image. Perhaps through some type of demonic involvement, the image will be given the ability to speak and give the order that all who refuse to worship the image are to be killed (Rev. 13:15). He will also force everyone to receive a mark, which will identify them as a worshiper of the beast. Without this mark, no one will be allowed to buy or sell (Rev. 13:15–16). The pressure to conform will be tremendous in that day. Only those with a genuine relationship with Christ will be able to stand under the pressure.

Then, John recorded that the number of the beast is man's number, 666. Again, much ink has been used in various detailed explanations of what this number represents. Honestly, the explanations I have read are not worth the paper upon which they were written. They are simply man's guesses.

When the day John is describing comes, I believe that Christians will be fully aware of what they are being asked to do. The Holy Spirit will give them insight into the situation. No believer will "mistakenly" take the mark of the beast. In that day, it will be very clear what they are being asked to do, and those who belong to the Lord will refuse to do so at all costs—even if it costs them their lives. For that reason, I don't believe it is profitable for us to "guess" what the mark of the beast will be. God will make that known as that time arrives.

CHAPTER TWENTY

BOLSTER THE TROOPS

(REVELATION 14:1-13)

In a masterful way, much like a painter of the caliber of Thomas Kinkade, God painted a series of stark contrasts to the images He had just revealed to John. While chapters twelve and thirteen revealed Satan's evil assault on the plans and people of God, chapter fourteen demonstrates how God's exit strategy and subsequent victory party will unfold. It was designed to be a bright ray of hope breaking through some of the darkest days of history. These contrasts are brilliant.

In contrast with the terrible trials and tribulations that believers will be required to endure, John was shown the grand celebration that will occur as believers are united with Christ (Rev. 14:1–5). Their severe persecution will be quickly forgotten as they join in the eternal victory celebration that is unlike anything the world has ever seen.

Those bearing the mark of God, as contrasted with those bearing the mark of the beast, will join in this celebration of God's deliverance. John was assured that all who had been sealed (represented by the number 144,000) would be present with God for the celebration. Not one of them would be left out, despite Satan's greatest efforts to the contrary. Through this scene, God was reassuring His followers that all the things they endured on earth would be worth it when they saw Him face to face in Heaven. Their joy would far outweigh the sufferings they had endured.

In the next scene, John saw three angels flying across the sky, each echoing the important message which God's people had shared with their world prior to Christ's return (Rev. 14:6–13). These would be the messages that would bring salvation to the believers and condemnation the unbelievers. These messages contained the truth that the world needed to hear, in contrast to the deceptive lies that the beast and the false prophet had spread. Each angel had a unique message.

The first angel proclaimed the eternal gospel, which included the need for man to repent and turn to God for salvation. Those who heard and responded by faith would be saved; the rest would be condemned. This must be done before the trumpets are complete, or it will be too late.

The second angel announced the coming destruction of the world system, which had seduced men to turn their backs on God. They were warned that the very things men place their trust in would soon crumble before their eyes. They should repent and look to God to be their supplier. This destruction will occur during the pouring out of the seven bowls of God's wrath.

The third angel warned of the penalty that will be inflicted upon those who worship the beast and take his mark. He warned that those who took that mark would experience the full fury of God's wrath and be tormented forever in Hell. They are warned that before taking Satan's mark they should carefully consider the consequences that await those who do. The inhabitants of the earth are warned that the punishment will not be temporary, but will last forever and ever. This punishment will commence as the lost are sentenced at the Great White Throne Judgment.

Because the stakes are so high, the saints of God are reminded to exercise patient endurance by obeying God's commands and remaining faithful to Jesus (Rev. 14:12). Blessings and eternal rest are pronounced from the heavens for those who die in their stand for the Lord, in contrast to the everlasting torment that awaits their foes who choose to follow Satan (Rev. 14:13).

CHAPTER TWENTY-ONE

THE VICTORS AND THE VANQUISHED

After showing John the events that led the world to the place of judgment, God took him right back to the two events that are linked to the seventh trumpet. With the sounding of that final trumpet, everything will dramatically change. The events linked to that moment are illustrated for John through the use of two distinct harvests. Not only would this information serve to encourage believers, but it would also serve to link the seven trumpets to the seven bowls as a master link serves to hold two pieces of chain together.

As John looked on, two harvest scenes were carried out. The first scene involved a grain harvest, which represents the gathering of the people of God into Heaven. This event is commonly referred to as the rapture of the Church.

The second scene involved the gathering and trampling of grapes in a huge winepress. This event pictured the great judgment of God upon the wicked inhabitants of the earth.

The first harvest depicts the calling of God's people out of this world. The second harvest shows the destruction that awaits those who lack a saving faith in Christ. In reality, the grape harvest is a concise word picture summarizing the terrible events of the seven bowls of wrath that John was about to witness.

In the gospel of Luke, Jesus reminded His followers how the events of that day would unfold. This is incredibly important to grasp at this point. Listen to Jesus' words:

> *Just as it was in the days of Noah, so also will it be in the days of the Son of Man. People were eating, drinking, marrying and being given in marriage up to the day Noah entered the ark. Then the flood came and destroyed them all. It was the same in the days of Lot. People were eating and drinking, buying and selling, planting and building. But the day that Lot left Sodom, fire and sulfur rained down from heaven and destroyed them all. It will be just like this on the day the Son of Man is revealed* (Luke 17:26–30).

In the days of Noah and Lot three things happened, one after the other. First, God warned the people of the coming judgment. Next, He removed His people from harms way. And then, immediately He destroyed all who were left behind. These same three things will occur in the end. Through the seals and the trumpets, God will warn the world to repent and turn to Him. Then, He will remove His people from the earth (rapture). And then, immediately He will destroy all who are left behind (bowls).

The two harvest scenes we are about to examine vividly depict these last two parts; thus, they follow naturally after the warning shots of the seven trumpets.

Grain Harvest (Rev. 14:14-16)

Let's begin by examining the first half of the drama. John recorded what he saw with these words:

> *I looked, and there before me was a white cloud, and seated on the cloud was one "like a son of man" with a crown of gold on his head and a sharp sickle in his hand. Then another angel came out of the temple and called in a loud voice to him who was sitting on the cloud, "Take your sickle and reap, because the time to reap has come, for the harvest of the earth is ripe." So he who was seated on the cloud swung his sickle over the earth, and the earth was harvested* (Rev. 14:14–16).

It was no mistake that God inserted this passage at this point. It belongs between the last trumpet and the first bowl because that is exactly when the rapture will occur in God's master plan. The rapture will occur in conjunction with the blowing of the last of the seven trumpets, before God pours out His bowls of wrath on the lost world.

Here, it is clothed in the imagery of a great harvest scene. Over and over again the New Testament uses this same imagery to depict the end of the age and the coming of Christ. Even some of Jesus' parables describe the end in this way. Notice the similarities between what John saw in his vision, and what the Bible promises will occur.

In this drama, John saw Jesus "seated on a cloud," swinging a mighty sickle, and harvesting the earth (Rev. 14:14, 16). Joel had promised a similar scene in the final days as recorded in Joel 3:12–16:

> *Let the nations be roused; let them advance into the Valley of Jehoshaphat, for there I will sit to judge all the nations on every side. Swing the sickle, for the harvest is ripe. Come, trample the grapes, for the winepress is full and the vats overflow—so great is their wickedness! Multitudes, multitudes in the valley of decision! For the day of the LORD is near in the valley of decision. The sun and moon will be darkened, and the stars no longer shine. The LORD will roar from Zion and thunder from Jerusalem; the earth and the sky will tremble. But the LORD will be a refuge for his people, a stronghold for the people of Israel.*

Jesus Himself had described a similar scene when He taught about the kingdom of Heaven and the final harvest of the earth in Mark 4:26–29:

> *This is what the kingdom of God is like. A man scatters seed on the ground. Night and day, whether he sleeps or gets up, the seed sprouts and grows, though he does not know how. All by itself the soil produces grain—first the stalk, then the head, then the full kernel in the head. As soon as the grain is ripe, he puts the sickle to it, because the harvest has come.*

Jesus had promised that the harvest would mark the end of the age, and the angels would serve as harvesters (Mt. 13:36–43). John was shown the same to be true through these two harvest scenes. Some object to this interpretation claiming that since Jesus is the one who *"swung his sickle over the earth"* that He was the sole harvester instead of the angels. They claim that Jesus' involvement would not fit the description offered in other places of the Bible. However, John was not trying to exclude the angels, but simply showing that Jesus was in charge of the harvest. Just as John was not intending to imply that a literal sickle would be used to cut down believers and gather them into a big bundle, neither was he intending to imply that Jesus was acting alone.

Let me illustrate how we might say the same type of thing in our day. It is very common to say that a farmer "harvested his crop" without meaning that he did all of the work alone. The truth is a farmer could rightfully claim to have harvested his crop by having the work done by those he has employed. The same type of thing could be understood through John's word picture. Jesus could rightfully be given credit for the harvest, even though His angels were allowed to participate in it.

Jesus stated that no one knew the hour of His return except for the Father (Mk. 13:32). In his vision, John witnessed an angel coming out of the temple—symbolizing the presence of God—communicating to Christ that the time had come to "reap" the fruit of His labor (Rev. 14:15). It was a dramatic way of saying that God had given the order for the harvest to occur. The angel that John heard was simply relaying the message of God with a loud voice for all to hear. The angel communicated the command, not for Jesus' sake, but for the rest of Heaven to hear, and for John to record. What John recorded was very similar to what Paul had written earlier:

> *For the Lord himself will come down from heaven, with a loud command, with the voice of the archangel and with the trumpet call of God, and the dead in Christ will rise first. After that, we who are still alive and are left will be caught up together with them in the clouds to meet the Lord in the air. And so we will be with the Lord forever* (1 Thess. 4:16–17).

Notice all the different elements mentioned by Paul that are also present in the harvest scene John recorded. The Lord Himself was present. There was a loud command with the voice of the archangel. The harvest is connected to the final trumpet call of God (the seventh trumpet). The dead in Christ and those Christians who are still alive will both be called up to meet the Lord in the air and be with Him forever. This scene in the book of Revelation perfectly fits what the Bible reveals in other places.

Jesus promised to come again to gather those who belonged to Him. He told His followers, *"If I go and prepare a place for you, I will come back and take you to be with me that you also may be where I am"* (John 14:3). Here, John saw one who looked *"like a son of man"* (Jesus' favorite title for Himself) coming on the clouds to gather His harvest. This description is a clear reference to Jesus gathering His followers.

The gospels also used the language of the harvest to depict the return of Christ in all of His glory. In the parable of the weeds (Mt. 13:24–30, 36–43) we are told that *"the harvest is the end of the age, and the harvesters are angels."* In Matthew's parable, the "servants" were told by their master to *"gather the wheat and bring it into [the] barn"* (Mt. 13:30). Jesus promised that *"He would send His angels with a loud trumpet call, and they will gather His elect from the four winds, from one end of the heavens to the other"* (Mt. 24:34). Jesus promised that all would *"see the Son of Man coming on the clouds of the sky, with power and great glory"* (Mt. 24:30; Mk. 13:26, 14:62). All of this imagery points to the scene John was witnessing on the heavenly stage.

John was also told something that would prove critically important. When the angel relayed the message for Jesus to reap His harvest, he explained why the time had finally come. The angel said, *"Take your sickle and reap, because the time to reap has come, for the harvest of the earth is ripe"* (Rev. 14:15). The word "ripe" literally means "dried up." It was complete! It was finished! Nothing more would be gained by waiting a minute longer.

The angel was communicating an incredibly important message we need not miss. At that moment in history, when God declares that the time has come for the rapture of Christians to take place, all of those who would ever come to Christ for salvation will have come. No other person would ever be added to the kingdom by postponing the harvest. At that moment, the roster of Heaven will be complete. There will no longer be any benefit for the children of God to remain on the earth. Their work of evangelism will be complete. The time will have come for them to be with their Savior for eternity. At that moment in history, God will never again draw another soul to Himself for salvation, and without His call, no one else can come (Jn. 6:44).

This message is critical because many, like me, were taught that if they somehow missed the rapture they would still be given another opportunity to repent and be saved. This passage makes it clear that when the rapture occurs, the harvest will be complete. The only thing that will remain to be accomplished will be for the enemies of God to be punished. There will be no further opportunities extended for people to repent. Those who have postponed their preparations will find themselves shut out of Heaven much like the foolish bridesmaids and the wicked servant Jesus described in Matthew 25.

The Grape Harvest (Rev. 14:17-20)

After the drama of the grain harvest had ended, John witnessed a grape harvest. In this drama, God showed John what would come of those who lacked a personal relationship with Christ. Here are the words John used to describe the scene that he saw:

> *Another angel came out of the temple in heaven, and he too had a sharp sickle. Still another angel, who had charge of the fire, came from the altar and called in a loud voice to him who had the sharp sickle, "Take your sharp sickle and gather the clusters of grapes from the earth's vine, because its grapes are ripe." The angel swung his sickle on the earth, gathered its grapes and threw them into the great winepress of God's wrath. They were trampled in the winepress outside the city, and blood flowed out of the press, rising as high as the horses' bridles for a distance of 1,600 stadia* (Rev. 14:17–20).

This scene depicts the day in which God's wrath will be poured out on the wicked. This harvest scene is a gruesome warning of the wrath of God that the enemies of God will endure following the rapture of the

Church. After removing His children from the earth, Christ will trample His enemies under His feet (Rev. 14:19–20, 19:15).

As this portion of the scene unfolded, an angel was seen coming out of the temple with a sharp sickle. Then, another angel came from the altar, and with a loud voice announced that the time for the grape harvest had arrived. This harvest was also declared "ripe," meaning that the time was precisely right for it to occur. There would be nothing else gained by postponing the event.

The scene depicts the grapes being gathered into a winepress and trampled underfoot. This was an image with which the people of John's day would have been very familiar. In that day when the grapes were harvested, they were placed in a large basin (winepress) with an attached trough that led down to a small collection basin. The grapes in the large basin would be trampled underfoot by those in the winepress until the juice flowed down the trough, filling up the collection basin. There, the juice would be collected and processed.

This practice was the basis for the scene acted out before John. It pictured the wicked being trampled under God's feet until their blood flowed freely into the streets. The enormity of the destruction was symbolized by the expression *"the blood flowed out of the press, rising as high as the horses' bridles for a distance of 1,600 stadia"* (Rev. 14:20). This description was probably not meant to be taken literally, but instead it was meant to serve as a gruesome description of the enormity of the devastation that would come upon all who had refused to submit themselves to God. The multitudes of people who have refused Christ's offer of redemption will find themselves the objects of God's wrath.

The Order of the Two Harvests

It is important to note the order of these two harvests. First, the harvest of the righteous will occur when the believers in Christ are gathered up to be with Christ (raptured). Some time soon after that, the harvest of the wicked will begin as God's wrath is poured out on the lost world through the seven bowl judgments. This will be followed by the return of Christ on a white horse with His followers riding close behind. In many ways, these scenes are reminiscent of an army general riding into town, gathering his troops, and heading out to battle. In that same way, Christ will come on the clouds and gather His children to Himself, before returning to earth to destroy His enemies.

It is later in the book of Revelation where John is shown this picture of Christ's return. In that scene, Jesus is seen wearing *"a robe dipped in blood"* and He is said to be *"treading the winepress of the fury of the wrath of God Almighty"* (Rev. 19:13, 15). This language unmistakably ties these two scenes together. The grape harvest will be concluded with the triumphant return of Christ. It is obvious that this event will take place after Christians have been raptured because Christ's followers are described as following close behind Him dressed in fine linen, white and clean (Rev. 19:14). That would not be possible if they were still living on the earth.

This order further illustrates that the Church will be removed before God's wrath is poured out on the lost world. Paul indicated this when he wrote: *"God did not appoint us to suffer wrath, but to receive salvation through our Lord Jesus Christ. He died for us so that, whether we are awake or asleep, we may live together with him"* (1 Thess. 5:9).

Even in the ancient world, the grape harvest would follow the grain harvest by about three months. The two harvests would not occur simultaneously, but as the grain harvest was completed, the time would draw near to begin the grape harvest. Therefore, it would not be correct for us to see these two events as happening simultaneously, but rather, back-to-back. That being the case, it makes perfect sense for the Church to be removed through the rapture (the grain harvest), and then for the bowls of God's wrath to be poured out on those who have refused God's offer of salvation (the grape harvest), the end of which will involve the return of Christ with His followers.

While the rapture will occur without warning, in the twinkling of an eye, at the sounding of the last trumpet (1 Cor. 15:52), the outpouring of God's wrath is never said to be completed so quickly. The process through which God's wrath will be poured out will not be a long, drawn-out process. However, it will be comprised of several consecutive events that will take a little time to execute. The pain associated with these events will probably make them seem a whole lot longer in duration than they actually are.

With these two harvest scenes fresh in John's mind, the seven angels with the seven last plagues took their places on the stage of Heaven.

SECTION SIX
THE THIRD WAVE

Having removed His Church from the earth, the time will have arrived for God to pour out His wrath upon His enemies—the ones who have rejected His incredible offer of forgiveness and salvation. For whatever reason, these remaining individuals will have neglected to prepare themselves for the second coming of Christ. As a result of their hard hearts and their unpreparedness, they will be left behind to endure the terrible wrath of God.

There is nothing about this next scene that is the least bit pretty. The pain and suffering is horrific. It is impossible for words to fully describe how terrible that day will be. No doubt, God had John record the intensity of the suffering to warn those who lacked a personal relationship with Jesus before it was too late.

In this section, you will get a glimpse of just how terrible those final days will be for those who lack saving faith in Jesus Christ. First, John describes the pouring out of the seven bowls of God's wrath. The magnitude of the suffering is almost incomprehensible. John follows this by showing the final demise of Satan's earthly kingdom. In those final days, God will be proven victorious as He destroys the worldly system and its deceptive leaders that Satan used to turn humanity's heart far from God.

Instead of understanding these two events as occurring one after the other, I believe they will occur simultaneously. In other words, as God's wrath is poured out, humanity will suffer greatly, and Satan's empire will be dismantled and destroyed. As the satanic empire comes crashing down, so will the hopes and dreams of those who have invested their lives in assuring its success. Just as a Louisiana fog evaporates under the heat of the morning sun, so will all hope of survival vanish in those final days.

CHAPTER TWENTY-TWO
CARPET BOMBING

Through the previous two harvest scenes, God made known to John His intent. He made it crystal clear that those belonging to God would be taken to Heaven, and those refusing His gracious offer of salvation would remain on the earth and suffer a degree of God's wrath previously unknown to humanity. In the next portion of Scripture, God zooms in from a wide-angle shot that shows a broad view of the end, to a tight shot that focuses on the finer details of that day.

Celebrating with Great Anticipation

The first detail that He brings to John's attention is the great celebration God's followers will enjoy as they are gathered to His side. Those who are victorious over the beast will be gathered around God's throne. They will be victorious, not because they somehow found a way to live though the persecution, but because they refused to compromise their faith and bow to the enemy of God. These victors will be gathered around a "sea of glass mixed with fire" where they will be rewarded with the very presence of God.

These worshipers will sing a song of deliverance to God. Their song will be similar to the song the Israelites sang upon their deliverance from Egypt. In fact, many of the things John was shown in this vision had ties to that momentous event in the Old Testament. The sea, the plagues, the song, the tent of the Testimony, and the destruction of God's enemies were all reminiscent of the Israelite's exodus from Egypt. John was communicating to his readers that the God who had proven Himself faithful to the Israelites, would also prove Himself faithful to the saints who overcome.

John was allowed to see inside the temple in Heaven as it was opened. If you will remember, at the conclusion of the seven trumpets, John had been allowed a glimpse into the temple (Rev. 11:19). Here, he is taken back to that same place. No doubt this vision served to link the bowls that were to follow with the trumpets that had preceded them. It was as if God was making sure John made the connection between the two series.

Tremendous Suffering (Rev. 15:1-16:1)

As mentioned earlier, the grape harvest would follow the grain harvest. Having removed His children from the earth, God would commence pouring out His wrath on those who remain. These seven bowls are part of that grape harvest. As John looked on, seven angels came from the temple prepared to carry out God's judgment on the lost world. They were given seven golden bowls of God's wrath, which they would soon pour out on the inhabitants of the earth. The time had come for unrepentant mankind to reap what he had sown. John watched as the seven angels with the seven final plagues prepared to pour them out upon the inhabitants of the earth. John was informed that these were to be the *"seven last plagues"* because *"with them God's wrath is completed"* (Rev. 15:1).

When these plagues begin, the temple will be filled with smoke representing God's glory and His power, and no one will be able to enter the temple until the seven plagues of the seven angels are completed (Rev. 15:8). Through this magnificent language, John is made keenly aware of the magnitude of this moment. As these events unfold, the glory and power of God will be displayed in such splendor that all of Heaven will be struck with awe. This day will give new meaning to the phrase "shock and awe." The pounding that the enemies of God will be forced to endure will be similar to a third-world country being carpet bombed by one of the world's superpowers. They will be unable to escape as wave after wave of attacks destroy their world.

John listened as a loud voice from within the temple ordered the seven angels to, *"Go, pour out the seven bowls of God's wrath on the earth"* (Rev

16:1). Unlike the seven seals and the seven trumpets, the order to "go" will not be repeated to each individual angel. In that day, one command will serve as the marching orders for all seven angels. As soon as one angel finishes the task of pouring out his bowl of wrath, the next angel will begin pouring out his bowl. The lingering effects of one judgment will not be complete before the next one begins. The inhabitants of the earth will barely have time to catch their breath before another judgment will come upon them. Make no mistake; this will be the most terrible time in human history.

Bowl One: (Rev. 16:2)

On cue, the first angel *"went and poured out his bowl on the land, and ugly and painful sores broke out on the people who had the mark of the beast and worshiped his image"* (Rev. 16:2). Similar to the first trumpet, this bowl was poured out on the land (earth). The resulting sores were reminiscent of the sores of the sixth Egyptian plague, which befell those who were the enemies of God. How terribly painful these sores will be on all who remain on the earth.

We are not told what will cause these sores, but we are told that they will be terribly painful for those who have taken the mark of the beast and worshiped his image. While it would be easy to assume that some type of nuclear or biological weapon will cause this type of injury, it is important to remember that these plagues will not be localized, or limited, to one geographical region of the world. Unlike a bomb that affects only one region of the world, these plagues will be inflicted worldwide, on all who remain on the earth. The suffering will be on a scale unlike anything this world has ever known.

One word of caution is in order here. While it is sometimes intriguing to speculate as to how mankind could create the great disasters that John writes about, it is important to remember that God will be in complete control of these events. The inhabitants of the earth will have no doubt that it is God pouring out His wrath upon them, and not just a world leader who has gone mad. While it is true that God could carry out His wrath through the use of human instruments, He could also just speak a command and every one of these events would occur without the assistance of any human being. If, in the beginning, God simply spoke and the worlds came into existence (and He did!), then He need do nothing more than speak and His creation would dissolve just the same. So, be careful not to get caught up trying to figure out how God will bring about these terrible disasters. Instead, realize He will do it in such a way that all will know that they are being forced to endure the terrible wrath of God.

Bowl Two: (Rev. 16:3)

The second angel followed immediately on the heels of the first. John reported that he *"poured out his bowl on the sea, and it turned into blood like that of a dead man, and every living thing in the sea died"* (Rev. 16:3). While the second trumpet wiped out one-third of the sea life, the second bowl caused complete destruction to every living thing in the sea. Allow the magnitude of that to sink in for just a moment.

In one fell swoop, everything living in the sea will be destroyed. John was witnessing destruction on a world-wide scale. This is not some oil spill that simply contaminates a portion of the sea and kills the marine life in that particular area. This is God's judgment being poured out in such a way that ALL sea life is destroyed. It is almost impossible for us to get our hands around devastation of this magnitude. There is no way for us to fully grasp the impact this event will have on the world's food supply. Try to imagine the horrific smell resulting from the dead marine life that will litter the shoreline. A major portion of the world's economy will be destroyed. Can you see how the destruction caused by the bowls of wrath will be interwoven into the demise of the economic system? You cannot separate the two.

Bowl Three: (Rev. 16:4–7)

The third angel was not far behind the second. He poured out his bowl of wrath on *"the rivers and springs of water and they became blood"* (Rev. 16:4). This time, instead of one-third of the fresh water supply becoming bitter—as in the case of the third trumpet—the entire fresh water supply will be turned to blood. No water filtration system in the world will be able to purify enough water for those living on the earth to drink enough water to survive when this occurs. The inhabitants of the earth will have nothing left to drink but blood. What a terrible fate for those who have rejected God.

John heard an angel proclaiming that God was just in His judgment because the inhabitants of the earth had shed the blood of God's saints and prophets. He reasoned that it was only appropriate for those who were set on shedding innocent blood to be forced to drink blood. Those at God's altar responded in agreement (Rev. 16:5–7).

Since mankind cannot live for long without drinkable water, it stands to reason that at this point in time humanity will not have many days left on this earth. This, once again, confirms the idea that the bowls will be poured out rapidly, one after the other.

Bowl Four: (Rev. 16:8–9)

The fourth angel poured out his bowl on the sun. This is similar to the fourth trumpet, which also impacted the sun (in addition to the moon and the stars). In the fourth trumpet, the light from the sun was dimmed. In the case of the fourth bowl, John saw just the opposite occurring. This time, the sun was *"given power to scorch people with fire"* (Rev. 16:8). The Bible records that the people will be *"seared by the intense heat"* to the point they will curse the name of God (Rev. 16:9). The heat in that day will be unbearable, and with no fresh water left to drink they will be unable to quench their thirst and rehydrate their bodies. The pain associated with dehydration will be intense, not to mention the other physical effects of the burning sun.

As their bodies suffer through the pain associated with these initial waves of God's wrath, they will continue to curse God. They will recognize the hand of God in these events, yet they will refuse to *"repent and glorify Him"* (Rev. 16:9). It is imperative to note that not one mention is made of anyone turning to God for salvation during these final moments of history. As in the parables Jesus taught, the opportunity for them to enter into a relationship with Him will be eternally lost. The time for repentance will be no more. Unable to turn to God, they will continue their verbal assault against Him.

Bowl Five: (Rev. 16:10–11)

The fifth angel will pour out his bowl on the throne of the beast and plunge his kingdom into darkness. The details of how this event will unfold are spelled out for John a little bit later (Rev. 17–18). For now, he is simply told the outcome. When that day comes, Satan's leaders, and the empire they have built, will begin to crumble. I will explain the demise a little bit later.

The fifth trumpet had brought the opening of the Abyss and the release of the demonic locusts. The result was the darkening of the sun and the sky and a time of torture for those lacking the mark of God. Those experiencing this torture sought death but could not find it.

During the fifth bowl of God's wrath, the inhabitants remaining on the earth will, once again, find themselves in the midst of great pain and suffering. The pain will be so great that they will *"gnaw their tongues in agony and curse the God of heaven because of their pains and their sores"* (Rev. 16:10–11). This description indicates that the effects of the first few bowls of wrath were still being felt even as the final bowls were being poured out.

John, once again, made it clear that even though the people going through these terrible times will recognize the hand of God in their suffering, they will continue to curse God instead of repenting of the evil they had done (Rev. 16:11). He is not saying that they should have repented, but he is simply recording what he witnessed in response to their suffering.

Those who think they will come to God on their own terms and in their own time are seriously mistaken. Apart from the prompting of God's Spirit, no one can turn to God for salvation (Jn. 6:44). When God's Spirit stops drawing people's hearts to God for salvation, they will find themselves unable to turn to God. All they will be able to do is to curse the God they have rejected. Those who had continually rejected God's offer of saving grace will find themselves as the recipients of His terrible wrath.

Bowl Six: (Rev. 16:12–16)

The sixth angel will pour out his bowl of wrath on the great river Euphrates, the same river mentioned in the sixth trumpet. During the time of the sixth trumpet, one-third of mankind was killed as four angels led a massive army armed with three deadly plagues. Here, in the sixth bowl, mankind was, once again, being gathered for a huge slaughter. The riverbed John saw was dried up, providing a pathway for the world's armies to travel as they gathered together for a great showdown. The dry river bed imagery could imply that the barriers (rivers) separating opposing nations will vanish as foes become allies in this final battle against God. In other words, former enemies could suddenly share a common goal of opposing God and His army.

This imagery could also be intended to remind the reader of the dry ground over which the Israelites traveled through the Red Sea as they fled Pharaoh's pursuing army. You will remember that as soon as the Israelites had crossed the sea and Pharaoh's army entered it, God closed the waters and drowned Pharaoh's army. The destruction was great. What Pharaoh saw as a pathway to victory quickly became a road to destruction. His army, in their quest to conquer, became the conquered, as they were baited into a trap from which they would not emerge alive. Perhaps John is communicating something of the same here.

During the sixth bowl, it becomes obvious that the dragon, the beast, and the false prophet form a demonic trinity. The dragon will proclaim himself to be God, the beast will try to take the place of Christ, and the false prophet will pretend to function as the Holy Spirit. John was a witness to froglike demons coming out of each of their mouths. These demons will use miraculous signs to convince the kings of the whole world to unite in this one final showdown with God. Winner will take all!

As all restraints are removed and their true colors are allowed to shine through, the kings of the world, possessing nothing but hatred for God, will agree to partner with the forces of evil to wage the war to end all wars. In a bold move, they will take on the army of God.

It is doubtful that God intended to imply that all of the armies of the world would literally be gathered in the same physical location, as that would seem logistically impossible. Instead, He seems to be implying that all the remaining members of the human race would be united by their common hatred of God. Already, they have been cursing God, now they are going to fight against Him.

So, in a real sense they would be united as one army in their quest to overthrow God and His kingdom. Thus, John was shown them coming together as a unified army in this great battle against God, a battle they were sure to lose! This is the battle commonly referred to as The Battle of Armageddon.

At this particular point in John's vision, God did not reveal the details of the battle that was to come; He simply set the stage for the showdown by uniting the troops. Later in the book of Revelation, John is told of this incredible showdown. There, John wrote:

> *I saw heaven standing open and there before me was a white horse, whose rider is called Faithful and True. With justice he judges and makes war. His eyes are like blazing fire, and on his head are many crowns. He has a name written on him that no one knows but he himself. He is dressed in a robe dipped in blood, and his name is the Word of God. The armies of heaven were following him, riding on white horses and dressed in fine linen, white and clean. Out of his mouth comes a sharp sword with which to strike down the nations. "He will rule them with an iron scepter." He treads the winepress of the fury of the wrath of God Almighty. On his robe and on his thigh he has this name written:* KING OF KINGS AND LORD OF LORDS. *And I saw an angel standing in the sun, who cried in a loud voice to all the birds flying in midair, "Come, gather together for the great supper of God, so that you may eat the flesh of kings, generals, and mighty men, of horses and their riders, and the flesh of all people, free and slave, small and great." Then I saw the beast and the kings of the earth and their armies gathered together to make war against the rider on the horse and his army. But the beast was captured, and with him the false prophet who had performed the miraculous signs on his behalf. With these signs he had deluded those who had received the mark of the beast and worshiped his image. The two of them were thrown alive into the fiery lake of burning sulfur. The rest of them were killed with the sword that came out of the mouth of the rider on the horse, and all the birds gorged themselves on their flesh* (Rev. 19:11–21).

When this battle occurs at the end, believers will accompany Christ, but make no mistake, the battle will be His. It is He who will strike down all those who oppose Him. It is He who will rule with an iron scepter. It is He who will capture the beast and the false prophet and cast them into the fiery lake of burning sulfur. Not one member of the Lord's army will be lost in this battle, but every human being opposed to God will be the object of God's wrath.

In this sixth bowl, John witnesses the opponents of God staging for this great showdown. They are digging in, absolutely convinced that they can somehow take on God and win. They were sadly mistaken. It will not be long before John will hear the battle cry of the angels of Heaven ring out signifying the beginning of the battle and the end of the opponents of God.

Bowl Seven: (Rev. 16:17–21)

The time had finally come for the seventh angel to pour out the final bowl of God's wrath into the air. Of the few who have managed to survive the first six bowls of wrath, not many will be able to survive this last one. As the angel poured out this final bowl of God's wrath, a loud voice came from the throne saying, *"It is done!"* This was the last of the plagues. This shout of victory was followed by flashes of lightning, rumblings, peals of thunder, and an earthquake more tremendous than any other earthquake since man has been on the earth (Rev. 16:17–18). The great city (a reference to man's civilization) split into three parts and collapsed (Rev. 16:19). God poured out the cup filled with the wine of the fury of His wrath on *"Babylon the Great"* (Rev. 16:19), a reference to the world system of that day.

The only way John could summarize the extent of the devastation he witnessed was to declare that every island fled and the mountains could not be found (Rev. 16:20). Huge hailstones of about a hundred pounds each were seen falling from the sky upon men. The plague was so terrible the inhabitants of the earth were, once again, heard cursing God (Rev. 16:21). One cannot help but notice the absence of repentance as God executes His final act of wrath upon those who have refused His gracious offer of salvation.

Now that John had been shown the order of the judgments, he was about to be shown how Satan's kingdom would rise to power before finally being plunged into darkness. God revealed the punishment that would be doled out upon the false religious system developed by Satan to lead the hearts of men far from God. God also revealed the demise of the worldly economic system, which Satan used to fund his false leaders and peddle his propaganda.

CHAPTER TWENTY-THREE

THE COLLAPSE OF THE WORLDLY EMPIRE

Before John was shown the final battle, which will occur when Christ and His army returns, he was shown how the satanic world empire, headed up by the beast, the false prophet, and the other corrupt world leaders, would be destroyed. Like a demolition crew with an oversized wrecking ball, God will dismantle Satan's empire piece by piece until there is nothing left but a pile of rubble. The demise of Satan's empire will take place as the bowls of God's wrath are poured out.

This satanic empire will be made up of a religious system as well as a commercial system. First, God showed John the demise of the religious system. Then, John was shown the collapse of the commercial system. Both are described in vivid detail.

The False Religious System (Rev. 17)

John used several different metaphors to describe the false religious system and the false leaders that Satan would work through as he seeks to turn the hearts of men far from God. Since these elements were combined into a single group, he often referred to them in the singular. John referred to them using many different metaphors: *"the great prostitute who sits on many waters"* (Rev. 17:1), *"a woman sitting on a scarlet beast"* (Rev. 17:3), *"Babylon the Great, the mother of prostitutes and of the abominations of the earth"* (Rev. 17:5), and *"the great city that rules over the kings of the earth"* (Rev. 17:18). She (the false religious system) is contrasted with the "woman" who gave birth to the Messiah back in Revelation chapter twelve.

The great prostitute (false religious system) was seen sitting on many waters—a metaphor indicating the great influence she will exert over the multitudes of lost people inhabiting the earth (Rev. 17:15). The kings of the earth are going to commit adultery with her, insinuating that she will have intimate ties with the political leaders of that day and that the politicians will use this false religious system for their own pleasure, promotion, and profit (Rev. 17:2). She will intoxicate all of the inhabitants of the earth (a reference to non-Christians) with the wine of her adulteries (Rev. 17:2) by telling them what their itching ears want to hear (2 Tim. 4:3). She will be carried along on the back of a scarlet beast (Satan's agent who will be described in more detail shortly). The fact that she will ride the scarlet beast illustrates that she will use him to get where she wants to go. For a time, both parties will help the other. The false religious system will benefit from the support it gains from the political system, and the political system will benefit from the support it gets from the false religious system. These two will make strange bedfellows . . . for a while.

The "woman" will be dressed in purple and scarlet, and will glitter with gold, precious stones, and pearls (Rev. 17:4). In other words, this religious system will be attractive, well financed, and very successful—all the things worldly people will long for in that day. Her success (further symbolized by the golden cup in her hand) will be used to detract attention away from her abominations and the filth of her adulteries (Rev. 17:4). People will focus on her success and overlook her shortcomings and the emptiness of her promises.

Like the prostitutes of John's day who wore headbands proclaiming their "sinful specialty," which made them so seductive, this false religion will proudly boast of its ability to deliver something for which the world longs—perhaps prosperity. The descriptive title John gave her was, *"Babylon the Great: The Mother of Prostitutes and of the Abominations of the Earth"* (Rev. 17:5). Babylon, used in this way, was not a reference to a geographical location, but instead it was meant to liken her back to the Babylon of old, which was the source (or center) of much of the false worship of the ancient world. John was saying that the false worship of the end-times will be very similar in nature to the false worship found in the ancient world. The fact that she is referred to as Babylon the Great shows the extent of the influence she will have in that day. In other words, in the final days, the false religious system will exercise great power and influence for Satan and his kingdom.

John noticed that she was *"drunk with the blood of the saints, the blood of those who bore testimony to Jesus"* (Rev. 17:6). Since the false religious system will be in direct contradiction to the truth of God's Word, it will do everything in its power to eliminate those who bear testimony to the truth of Jesus Christ. This aligns perfectly with the issuing of the mark of the beast and the martyrdom that follows. By killing those who proclaim the truth, she will seek to silence any voice opposing her deceptive message. This martyrdom of Christians is what John was referring to in this passage.

John reported being "greatly astonished" by the great prostitute (Rev. 17:6) and her close ties with the political system of that day (the beast she was riding). He does not say that he was astonished at her appearance, her power over the people, the deceptiveness of her ways, or her influential circle of friends, but at her relationship with the beast. It was a combination John had a hard time reconciling in his mind. The angel noticed his astonishment and offered John an explanation concerning the beast.

The scarlet beast the woman rode was described as a beast that *"once was, now is not, and will come up out of the Abyss and go to his destruction"* (Rev. 17:8). This same description is offered in reference to the one commonly known as the antichrist. This description of the antichrist is a reference to the faked death and resurrection that he will use as a tool to convince the world of his great power. This manufactured miracle will cause the non-Christian inhabitants of the earth, whose names have not been written in the Book of Life, to be astonished when they look upon the "resurrected beast" (Rev. 17:8). It is likely that Satan will use his demonic powers to pull off this great "pseudo-miracle." The fact that the beast will seem to have suffered a fatal head wound and somehow come back to life will be proof enough for the deceived multitudes that he is worthy to be followed. They will be enamored by the "proof" he presents without considering the source of that proof.

John was told that the seven heads of the beast were symbolic of *"seven hills on which the woman sits"* (Rev. 17:9). John's contemporaries would have understood that phrase as a reference to Rome, the center of emperor worship and idolatry. This indicates that the beast will be enamored with himself, and he will expect the rest of the world to feel likewise. In one form or another, he will reinstitute a form of emperor worship, which John has already touched on in relation to the mark of the beast (Rev 13:11–18).

In the next verse, John was told that the seven heads also represented "seven kings" (Rev. 17:10). Of those seven kings, he was told that five of them had fallen, one is, and one is yet to come. Then, the angel explained that the beast was going to be an eighth king, yet he *"belongs to the seven"* (Rev. 17:11). Most likely this meant that the final leader would have ties to one of the wicked leaders of the past in some way or another. Much speculation has been made about this, but I have no way to know for sure, so I will refrain from speculation.

The ten horns represent *"ten kings who have not yet received a kingdom, but who for one hour will receive authority as kings along with the beast"* (Rev. 17:12). In the day when the antichrist rises to power, there will be many new national leaders who will be enamored by this individual. While their reigns will not last long, they will be critical to the success of the beast. These ten leaders will give their power and authority to the beast and together they will wage war against the Lamb (Rev. 17:14). Despite their great alliance, it was made clear to John that they would not be successful in their war against the Lamb because Christ is *"the Lord of lords and the King of kings"* (Rev. 17:14).

John noticed that in this upcoming battle, Christ would not return to fight alone. He would bring with Him *"His called, chosen, and faithful followers"* (Rev. 17:14). He was referring to the battle that will occur when Christ returns riding on a white horse with the armies of Heaven following behind Him (Rev. 19:11–21). As I mentioned earlier, that battle will be over before it begins. Christ will demolish His opponents despite their greatest efforts to the contrary. They will prove to be no match for Him.

John was told that when the beast was through using the prostitute (false religious system), he and the other world leaders would turn and devour her. They would hate her, bring her to ruin, leave her naked, eat her flesh, and burn her with fire (Rev. 17:16). In other words, the political branch of evil would turn on the religious branch of evil. The "player" would be played. Those false religious leaders who had ridden Satan's powerful machine for their own profit will discover that they had simply been used by him to carry out his own agenda. Their hypocrisy will be exposed, and they will be brought to ruin in full view of the world. Most likely this will be done by the beast to convince the world that religion is a hoax and only he can be trusted.

When the false religious system has finished serving Satan's purpose he will discard it like a pimp discards a used up, nonprofitable prostitute. Having served his purpose, her true identity will be exposed for all to see. All she had been promised will be stripped away. She will be left desolate and despised, further illustrating that evil alliances are fickle at best, deadly at worse.

In what will be a neurotic, self-aggrandizing move, the beast will methodically eliminate all who stand a chance at siphoning away any of the worship others might offer to him—even if that means destroying one of his own. By exposing the false religious system that the people had grown to trust, he will posture himself as the only one who can be trusted to care for the people's best interests. He hopes this will help him capture the people's full devotion. His exposure of the false religious system will not be done in an effort to protect the people from the lies of the false religious system, but it will be done in order to promote a grander lie: that he is the savior of the world, the only one who deserves the worship of all men. What an abomination to God!

God reminds John that no matter how grand Satan's schemes may seem, God is actually the one who is working out an even grander plan. Satan will think that he is calling the shots, when in reality God is in complete control. The angel confirmed this when he told John, *"God has put it into their hearts* (the ten kings) *to accomplish his purpose by agreeing to give the beast their power to rule, until God's words are fulfilled"* (Rev. 17:17). So, even when it looks like Satan has cooked up a plan to favorably position himself, God remains sovereign.

The Commercial System (Rev. 18)

After watching the beast devour the false religious leaders, John was shown the coming collapse of the political and economic system that the satanic leaders will have worked so hard to create. Again, the title "Babylon the Great" was applied to this system indicating that it will be part of Satan's empire. The coming collapse of this empire is so certain that the angel described its demise as if it had already occurred: *"Fallen! Fallen is Babylon the Great!"* (Rev. 18:2). What will appear to be unshakable will inevitably become nothing more than a *"home for demons and a haunt for every evil spirit"* (Rev. 18:2). I will explain this phrase in more detail when we get to the thousand-year reign.

The angel warned John of how sinful the world will become in those final days. In those days, the nations of the earth will go crazy in their quest to be self-sufficient, even if that requires them to enter into some pretty unholy alliances. In describing that day yet to come, the angel told John, *"All the nations have drunk the maddening wine of her adulteries. The kings of the earth have committed adultery with her, and the merchants of the earth grew rich from her excessive luxuries"* (Rev. 18:3). The nations will have bought into Satan's system lock, stock, and barrel, only to watch as that system crumbles before their eyes.

Another angel joined in the drama to warn believers to stay far away from this commercially prosperous but morally bankrupt system. He urgently pled with God's people, *"Come out of her, my people, so that you will not share in her sins, so that you will not receive any of her plagues, for her sins are piled up to heaven, and God has remembered her crimes"* (Rev. 18:4–5). Christians are warned not to get caught up in this worldly system, because the day will come when all who are a part of it will suffer ruin. Believers are to look to God, not the world's system, to define their lives and to discover their worth. John warns believers, not because they will be present when it collapses, but so they will not place their hope in something that is sure to crumble.

Almost in mid-sentence the angel switched from addressing John to crying out to God for vengeance on this wicked world system. He pled for God to do unto the wicked world system as she had done unto God's people. The angel longed for God to pay her back double for all the harm she had inflicted on the Church. He was eager for God to silence the arrogant heart that proudly boasted of her position, her protection, and her lasting joy (Rev. 18:7).

The angel then reported how swiftly the demise of the evil world system would come. It will seem that out of nowhere, God will step in and set the record straight. He will remove His children and pour out His wrath. The angel promised, *"In one day her plagues will overtake her: death, mourning and famine. She will be consumed by fire, for mighty is the Lord God who judges her"* (Rev. 18:8). John was promised that God's judgment will come swiftly and completely.

When that judgment comes, all those who are invested in that system will respond to its demise. The kings of the earth who have committed adultery with her will weep and mourn and be terrified that they were associated with her (Rev. 18:9–10). Perhaps they fear that the same punishment she had received now awaits them. It does!

The land merchants and the sea merchants will mourn because there will be no one left to buy their merchandise (Rev. 18:11–19). It is not that they cared deeply for her; instead, they will mourn because they will have lost their largest corporate account. Even their reason for mourning reveals the condition of their hearts—consumed with little more than love for themselves.

While the inhabitants of the earth mourn over the destruction of the system upon which they built their entire lives, those who resisted her seductive influence and her promise of prosperity are told to rejoice. The angel exclaimed, *"Rejoice over her, O Heaven! Rejoice saints, apostles and prophets! God has judged her for the way she treated you"* (Rev. 18:20).

Next, a "mighty angel" was seen hurling a large boulder into the sea symbolizing the violent end of the satanic world system. The angel used very descriptive language to let it be known that this was not a temporary setback to Satan's agenda, but it marked the end of his reign. He promised that the great city of Babylon would sink like a huge boulder, never to be found again (Rev. 18:21). Music would never be heard in the city again (Rev. 18:22). No workman of any trade would ever be found in it again (Rev. 18:22). With the use of multiple metaphors, he makes it clear that the worldly system will be crushed, never to rise again (Rev. 18:22–24).

With this announcement, the heavens erupted in praise, and a great worship service broke out as God judged the wicked world (Rev. 19). Nothing could silence their voices. Their endurance had paid off. Their enemy was crushed. Their blood had been avenged. Their God would now reign in all of His glory!

Let the Celebration Begin! (Rev. 19:1-10)

As Christ dismantled the system and its leaders, who have for so long opposed His rule, all of Heaven broke out in joyful shouts of praise. The inhabitants of Heaven celebrated His victory over evil and rejoiced as the invitation to the wedding supper of the Lamb was issued. John was told that Jesus' bride would be adorned in bright, clean, fine linen, which will be given to her as a symbol of her righteous acts. Then, the angel told John to write: *"Blessed are those who are invited to the wedding supper of the Lamb!"* (Rev. 19:9). Make no mistake; this will be an "invitation only" event. Not one of the saints in attendance will have purchased their own ticket. They will all be the recipients of God's gracious gift of salvation.

John was so caught up in the splendor of the moment he fell at the angel's feet and began to worship. The angel quickly redirected his worship to God, and reminded him to hold on to the testimony of Jesus (Rev. 19:10). All of the spectacular events that John had just witnessed fit perfectly into the timeline that Jesus had given to His disciples. It is for this reason that I suggested at the beginning of this book that we begin with Jesus' map of the end-times and allow the other biblical authors to color within His lines. The angel seems to be telling John to do the same.

CHAPTER TWENTY-FOUR

TOTAL ANNIHILATION

(REVELATION 19:11-21)

As a gifted communicator who paints multiple pictures to etch the main points of his message into the hearts of his audience, God paints one more picture of the great day in which Christ will defeat His foes on the earth. This time, God shows Christ mounted on a white horse, with fire in His eyes, justice in His heart, and many crowns on His head (Rev. 19:11–12). His robe has been dipped in blood, and His faithful followers form the heavenly army that follows closely behind him. Out of His mouth comes a sharp sword with which He will strike down the nations. He will rule them with an iron scepter as He *"treads the winepress of the fury of the wrath of God"* (Rev. 19:15). The birds of the air are even invited to come and to feast upon the flesh of those about to be killed in His wake. None will be spared, no matter their rank or their status (Rev. 19:18).

Those on the earth will try to "dig in" as they prepare to make war against the One on the white horse, but they will not be the least bit successful. Their leaders—the antichrist and the false prophet—will be captured and thrown alive into the fiery lake of burning sulfur (Rev. 19:19–20). Then the rest of those who oppose Christ will be killed with the sword that comes out of His mouth, and all of the birds of the air will gorge themselves on their flesh (Rev. 19:21).

With this vivid picture, God forever burns into the minds of His followers the truth that He will have the final word, and He will be the King of kings and the Lord of lords. No one can stand against Him for long.

The message could not be clearer to John and his future readers. The battle at the end won't even be close. Christ will conquer His every foe. Not one of them will be able to stand against Him in that day. It is also clear that Christ is not going to need the help of His great army. He will do all the work Himself, while His followers simply look on with amazement. Although His robe is dipped in blood, the robes of His followers will remain white and clean (Rev. 19:14).

SECTION SEVEN

MOPPING UP AND HEADING HOME

The last three chapters of Revelation reveal the mop-up operations and the return home of the faithful troops of God. In this final section, John will witness God exerting total dominion over all of His creation, even those things in the heavenly realm. Nothing in all of creation will be outside of His rule and reign.

First, John is shown the thousand-year reign of Christ. Then, he is shown the Great White Throne Judgment. Following that event, he is allowed to catch a glimpse of the new heaven and the new earth that will come down from God. Finally, John will hear Jesus say, *"Behold, I am coming soon!"* (Rev. 22:7).

CHAPTER TWENTY-FIVE

COSMIC CONFLICT

(REVELATION 20:1-10)

I promised you in the beginning of this book that when I felt I had reached a portion of Scripture that I was not sure how to interpret, I would admit my shortcomings. Revelation 20:1–10 (the thousand-year reign of Christ) has presented me with my greatest challenge.

Following the total annihilation of the earth's population, John is told of the thousand-year period during which Satan will be bound with a chain and cast into the bottomless pit so that he can no longer deceive the nations. During this thousand-year period, Christ, along with the believers who have been resurrected and given His authority, will reign. At the end of the thousand-year period, Satan will be released from his prison for a short time in order to go out and deceive the nations. Those he deceives will be gathered together into a massive army whose numbers will be like the sands of the seashore. They will launch an all-out attack against God and His children, before being ultimately defeated by God. At the time of their defeat, the multitude will be destroyed by fire from Heaven, and Satan will be cast into the lake of fire where the antichrist and the false prophet have been thrown. There they will remain for all of eternity (Rev. 20:1–10).

At first glance it sounds simple, doesn't it? That is what I thought! However, the more one studies the passage, the more evident it becomes that it is not so clear cut. Several problems present themselves almost immediately.

The question must be asked, "How should one interpret John's language?" Was it meant to be understood literally, or symbolically? One group insists that John's language was purely symbolic and that he was simply speaking of an undetermined period of time between Christ's ascension and His second coming. In other words, the language is symbolic of what Christ will be doing between His first coming and His second coming. They do not view the thousand-year reign as an actual event that follows chronologically after Christ returns to conquer His foes. The main problem with this interpretation is that it overlooks the fact that Satan is not yet bound and is still able to deceive the world. In fact, Scripture teaches believers: *"Be self-controlled and alert. Your enemy the devil prowls around like a roaring lion looking for someone to devour. Resist him, standing firm in the faith, because you know that your brothers throughout the world are undergoing the same kind of sufferings"* (1 Pet. 5:8–9). For that reason, this view is not acceptable to me.

Another group, at the other end of the theological spectrum, insists that the passage be interpreted in a strictly literal fashion, which seems to be ignorant of the fact that symbolism is used throughout the passage. For example, John states that Satan is bound with a chain and cast into a pit that has no bottom but does have a lid and a lock. Is there a literal chain that can hold demonic beings, or a literal pit with no bottom but a lid and a lock? While this vivid language communicates God's intended message, it is virtually impossible to take it literally.

I believe it is possible to occupy a middle ground, between these two extremes, without throwing conservative Christian theology out the window. In fact, I think it is the most theologically responsible thing one can do. Here is how that can work. One can understand the thousand-year reign as a literal thousand-year event that will follow chronologically after the defeat of Christ's enemies, and yet do so with the full understanding that John has used symbolic language to describe the details of that event. This is the very same principle that has been employed throughout the rest of the book of Revelation.

Even when one does what I have suggested, there are still many questions that arise, which must be dealt with. Some will be easy to answer, while others will have to wait for further revelation from God. Here are some of the most common questions I have encountered.

Why, if Jesus has just defeated and destroyed all of His earthly enemies (chapter 19), would He not finish the task and immediately defeat Satan and cast him into the lake of fire with the antichrist and the false prophet? Why would He choose to wait a thousand years? Why would He give Satan another opportunity to rebel against the Lord's authority and lead others to do the same?

Another group of intriguing questions concern the actual reign of Christ with His chosen followers. Over whom will they reign if all of Jesus' enemies were just slaughtered? If I am reading chapter 19 correctly, there will be no human beings alive on the earth over which they could reign. If all believers were raptured after the seventh trumpet, and all nonbelievers were destroyed by Christ as He returned riding on the white horse (chapter 19), then no humans will be left on the earth for Christ to reign over. Then, one must question, "Who will make up the huge army that Satan gathers together after his release from the pit, and from where will these individuals suddenly appear?" If this portion of Scripture was meant to be understood chronologically, it is hard to avoid the questions: "Who will be left on the earth?" and "How will they manage to survive on a decimated planet for a thousand years?"

These questions lead us to another question: "Where will Christ and His followers reign since the ecosystem of the earth has just been systematically dismantled to the point that it seems uninhabitable?" While I am aware that God will "make all things new," that renewal is not scheduled to occur until later (chapter 21), after Satan has been cast into Hell.

The questions are many and the answers are not easy to come by. In fact, with each set of "answers" that I found, several more questions surfaced. The truth is I have yet to find another author who has written a rock-solid solution that I can pass on to you.

As I have wrestled with this dilemma for the past year, I have formulated one possibility that I believe has merit. I wish I could tell you that the experts all agree with what I am about to reveal to you, but I must be honest and admit that I have not come across this in any of my research. That does not mean that I am the first to think it, but simply that I am not familiar with anyone else who has published these thoughts. It is entirely my own understanding of the thousand-year reign, but I think it answers many of the questions that have arisen throughout my research. Please prayerfully consider this possibility.

John says that Satan will be bound in such a way that he is unable to deceive the nations for the entire time he is bound (Rev. 20:3). Then, John reports that when Satan is released he will immediately go out and deceive the nations, which are scattered around the world (Rev. 20:7–8). Most of us naturally interpret the term "nation" as a gathering of people in one geographical area. However, the Greek word for "nation" that is used in this particular place in Scripture is the word *ethnos*, which we examined earlier. You will remember that this word referred to those with a different racial or religious profile. In its most literal sense, the plural uses of the word (nations) means anyone who is "non-Israel." This understanding applied to John's context would mean that he was speaking of anyone who was "non-Christian." Some sources would call them "pagans or heathens." In other words, they are those who choose not to submit to Christ.

So, what if those who remained on the earth—those whom Christ will rule with an iron scepter, those who Satan will gather together after his release from the bottomless pit—what if those nations were not "human nations" but instead, "demonic nations" made up of the fallen angels that originally rebelled with Satan?

Before you discount my suggestion, consider this. While describing the demolition of Satan's worldly empire, God sent an angel to proclaim, *"Fallen! Fallen is Babylon the Great! She has become a home for demons and a haunt for every evil spirit"* (Rev. 18:2). In this announcement, I believe God was telling us that the only ones who will remain on the earth after He destroys His earthly enemies will be the demons and the evil spirits. God even goes as far as to state that *"she will be consumed by fire, for mighty is the Lord God who judges her"* (Rev. 18:8). This is the same fate that awaits those who will be destroyed after Satan is released from the bottomless pit (Rev. 20:9).

To add further weight to this argument we should recall that Paul stated in 1 Corinthians 6:3 that we will one day judge angels. Surely he was not speaking of heavenly angels who did not rebel against God, but rather the fallen angels who did rebel and now await judgment. Could it be that Christians will reign over these fallen angels during the millennium?

Also, you should consider this: the fate of every other group of beings has been accounted for in John's storyline. By this point in time, the

Christians will have been raptured and returned to earth to rule with Christ. The antichrist and the false prophet will have been captured and cast into Hell. The surviving non-Christians will have been killed when Christ returned with His heavenly army. Finally, Satan will have been chained and cast into the bottomless pit for his thousand-year sentence. The only group that has not been accounted for is the fallen angels (demons and evil spirits). If this is not the group that Jesus and the saints will rule over, then what ever came of them?

Jesus taught that they would eventually end up in Hell (Mt. 25:41), but apart from this passage, we have not been told how they end up there. I believe John is informing us of their final rebellion and their eternal fate in this section. These fallen angels are the ones over whom Christ and His followers will reign. They will be the multitude numbered as the grains of sand who will join with Satan for one last stand against God, when Satan is released from the bottomless pit.

Stay with me! While Satan is bound, the demons will be left without their main leader. We know from Scripture that Christ has complete authority over them, and He has extended that authority to His followers. These fallen foes must do exactly as He commands. So, is it totally unrealistic to think that Christ and His followers will rule these demons with an iron scepter for a thousand years? Is it unimaginable to reason that after being subjected to Christ's rule for a thousand years that they would be mad as hornets and would want to seek revenge on God and His followers? Is it not a perfect ending to the storyline for the demons and their leader to be cast into the lake of fire after their final uprising against God? I think not! In fact, I think all of these things fit this context perfectly.

If my theory is accurate, then most of the questions I have raised above would be answered. The reason for the thousand-year delay would be to demonstrate to His followers that God, and His followers who have been given His authority, have complete authority over the demonic world. Furthermore, demons do not require a fully functional earth with the same environmental standards as humans in order to survive. Their presence on the scene does not have to be "manufactured," (as other theories must do to have someone for Christ to reign over) as they will already be present. The demonic beings are required to yield to Christ's absolute authority for as long as Christ requires them to do so. Plus, this theory would explain what will happen to the demons, whose fate is otherwise omitted from the storyline. Perhaps I am mistaken in this, but it is worth thinking about. I understand that there is no way for me to prove this theory to be true, but it sure seems to clear up a lot of the questions that otherwise remain unanswered.

What if God included this thousand-year period to clue us in on the fact that when everything seems to be over, it will not yet be over? What if this passage was included to inform us of His total dominion over, and destruction of, those who oppose Him in the spiritual realm?

While this two-paragraph passage of Scripture does not supply us with all of the details we might desire, it does clue us in on what God has in store immediately following His triumphant return. Perhaps God was just giving us a "heads up" that He has something unique planned for Satan and his minions before He once-and-for-all sentences them to an eternity in Hell. Perhaps we will one day understand it more completely. Maybe this was one of the many things on Paul's mind when he penned the words: *"Now we see but a poor reflection as in a mirror; then we shall see face to face. Now I know in part; then I shall know fully, even as I am fully known"* (1 Cor. 13:12). I am okay with that. I hope you are as well.

Despite any of our unanswered questions, one thing is certain: Christ will return and defeat Satan and all of his followers, and He will cast them into the eternal lake of fire where they will be tormented day and night for ever and ever (Rev. 20:10). I can live with that assurance even if questions about how He will accomplish it linger in my mind.

CHAPTER TWENTY-SIX

JUDGMENT DAY!

After the events of the thousand-year reign are concluded, God will issue a summons to every person who has lived and died apart from His saving grace. John was shown a courtroom drama that represented what that terrible day would be like.

John was shown that the dead, great and small, will be ordered to appear before God as He sits upon His Great White Throne in that day. These individuals will have no choice but to come. John's language makes it clear that every lost person will have to appear before God when he emphasizes that *"the sea gave up the dead that were in it, and Death and Hades gave up the dead that were in them, and each person was judged according to what he had done"* (Rev. 20:13). It is worth noting where these individuals will come from. They will come from the "sea," which is a metaphor for "the place of the dead," a place sometimes called the Abyss. Notice that Death and Hades will have to release their grip on those they have held bound. Most Bible scholars will agree that no Christians will be at this event. This judgment will be for nonbelievers only.

This will be a terrible day as God hands down His verdict and each defendant's eternal fate is sealed. There will be no appeals process, for God's judgment will be fair and just; besides, there is no higher court to which one may appeal.

As John was shown this day, he was made aware of a set of books and also a single book that would be used during the trial (Rev. 20:12). John wrote: *"The dead were judged according to what they had done as recorded in the books"* (Rev. 20:12). Evidently, God will use this set of books to present Heaven's case against the defendants. He will have undisputable evidence that each one of them fell short of the mark He had established for them. Every single one of them will be proven to be sinners. In short, there will be no denying that they were less than perfect and deserving of eternal death and damnation. One by one, each person will be judged *"according to what they had done"* while alive on the earth (Rev. 20:12–13). There will be no loopholes in that day. His case against them will be rock solid.

Having made His case against each of these individuals, God will then turn to the single book and make a careful search before handing down His final verdict. He will be searching the book known as the Book of Life (Rev. 20:12). Having pronounced them guilty of their shortcomings, God will look to see if their names are recorded in the Book of Life. Only if their name was recorded in this book would they be able to obtain the mercy and grace necessary to have their case against them dismissed. Of course, their names will not be in this book, for this book only contains the names of those who turned to God through faith in Jesus Christ. Their presence at this trial is evidence enough that they had not done so. Those who failed to turn to God through faith in Jesus Christ have never had their names recorded in this book. John tells his readers of the eternal significance of failing to make that decision when he wrote: *"If anyone's name was not found written in the book of life, he was thrown into the lake of fire"* (Rev. 20:15).

Reading this passage, one can understand how vital a relationship with God through faith in Jesus Christ is going to be. No one will be admitted into Heaven without it. No one!

This might be the perfect time for you to consider whether or not you have established such a relationship with God. If you have not, you should seriously consider doing so. Eternity hangs in the balance. You do not want to one day find yourself standing before this Judge.

CHAPTER TWENTY-SEVEN

MISSION ACCOMPLISHED!

Having been shown all that awaits those who failed to turn to God for salvation, John was allowed to see what awaits those who *do* belong to God. Talk about a study in contrasts. John was about to be shown a glimpse of the things God had waiting for him and all who faithfully follow God.

As John stood wide-eyed gazing into Heaven, he was shown the new heaven and the new earth that is to come (Rev. 21:1). He saw the Holy City—the New Jerusalem—coming down out of Heaven. It was adorned as a bride beautifully dressed for her husband (Rev. 21:2). A loud voice from the throne announced that the dwelling of God was now with men (Rev. 21:3). They will forever be His people, He will forever be their God, and He will live among them (Rev. 21:3). God Himself will *"wipe every tear from their eyes"* and *"there will be no more death or mourning or crying or pain, for the old order of things has passed away"* as God makes all things new (Rev. 21:4).

Even as John was taking in all that God has planned for His followers, God interrupted the tour to have John record one final contrast between those who are His and those who are not. He said to John:

> *I am the Alpha and the Omega, the Beginning and the End. To him who is thirsty I will give to drink without cost from the spring of the water of life. He who overcomes will inherit all this, and I will be his God and he will be my son. But the cowardly, the unbelieving, the vile, the murderers, the sexually immoral, those who practice magical arts, the idolaters and all liars—their place will be in the fiery lake of burning sulfur. This is the second death* (Rev. 21:6–8).

Could the outcome of the two groups be any clearer? Can you hear God's heart crying out to the lost world? It is as if He were saying, "If you will come to Me, I will give you all of this, but if you refuse, your eternal destiny will be far different. Choose carefully!" This break in the heavenly tour reminds us that God is not *"slow in keeping his promise, as some understand slowness. He is patient . . . not wanting anyone to perish, but everyone to come to repentance"* (2 Pet. 3:9).

Following the warning, the tour resumes. John is shown the marvelous city of God, in its full splendor. The scene is breathtaking. The magnificence of Heaven is described in the most glorious images that a person of John's day could imagine. The foundations, the streets, the walls, the gates—they are all described with images that one's mind can hardly comprehend.

The only thing that seems to be missing, at least in John's Jewish mind, is the temple. John states, *"I did not see a temple in the city, because the Lord God Almighty and the Lamb are its temple. The city does not need the sun or the moon to shine on it, for the glory of God gives it light, and the Lamb is its lamp"* (Rev. 21:22–23). When one has a face-to-face fellowship with God, there is no longer any need for a man-made temple.

This place God has prepared for His followers will be perfect, and those who inhabit it will have been made perfect through the work of Christ Jesus. It is written: *"Nothing impure will ever enter it, nor will anyone who does what is shameful or deceitful, but only those whose names are written in the Lamb's book of life"* (Rev. 21:27).

John was shown the river of the water of life that will flow from the heavenly throne down the middle of the great street of the city. He saw the tree of life that will be constantly yielding its fruit and bringing healing to all. The curse that resulted from the fall of mankind will have been lifted, and God's followers will have a face-to-face fellowship with God as they serve Him and reign with His Son for ever and ever (Rev. 22:1–6). John concludes God's great revelation with another grand announcement from Christ:

> *Behold, I am coming soon! My reward is with me, and I will give to everyone according to what he has done. I am the Alpha and the*

> *Omega, the First and the Last, the Beginning and the End. Blessed are those who wash their robes, that they may have the right to the tree of life and may go through the gates into the city. Outside are the dogs, those who practice magic arts, the sexually immoral, the murderers, the idolaters and everyone who loves and practices falsehood. I, Jesus, have sent my angel to give you this testimony for the churches. I am the Root and the Offspring of David, and the bright Morning Star. The Spirit and the bride say, "Come!" And let him who hears say, "Come!" Whoever is thirsty, let him come; and whoever wishes, let him take the free gift of the water of life* (Rev. 22:12–17).

With their mission complete on this earth, God calls His children to come home, and not to just any ordinary home. He calls them to come and inhabit the place especially prepared for them. Knowing that all of this awaits him and the other faithful followers, John cannot contain himself. He cries out, *"Amen. Come, Lord Jesus"* (Rev. 22:20). We should join our voices with his!

With this scene complete, the curtain closes on the book of Revelation. God's children are finally home with Him for eternity. Those who have opposed Him have been sentenced to an eternity in Hell. Perhaps the worst thing about Hell is not the fire, but the fact that the people confined there will forever live outside the presence of the loving God who created them. They will forever suffer the consequence of having not prepared themselves to meet God face to face.

CHAPTER TWENTY-EIGHT
BATTLE SUMMARY

When I stop and think about all that God has planned for those final days, it gets me excited! Now, I am not excited that Christians will suffer and die. And, I am not excited that the lost world will be condemned to Hell. However, I am excited that evil will finally be eliminated. Following those days, there will be no more pain, suffering, or sin for those of us who belong to God. Finally, the old order of things will pass away, and we will get to dwell in the presence of God for ever and ever. I cannot wait for that day.

I know that the days between now and then will not be easy ones, but the God who called us to Himself will strengthen us and prepare us to stand. That preparation must begin now. If you already have a personal relationship with God, you should continue to grow in your faith so that you will be able to stand firm when things get difficult. If you do not yet have that personal relationship with God, I wish you would contact me so we can discuss how you might get prepared for the day. You can email me at exitstrategy@ImpactEternityNow.org.

As we move closer and closer to the day of Christ's return, the Bible makes it clear that the number of deceivers will greatly increase. There will be men and women who claim to have a word from God, but in reality they will be little more than tools in the hand of Satan. You need to be familiar with the Word of God so that you can distinguish truth from error. As Jesus taught us, *"Watch out that no one deceives you. For many will come in my name, claiming, 'I am the Christ' and will deceive many"* (Mt. 24:4–5). Don't be one of the ones who are led astray. Test everything by comparing it to the Word of God. Cling to that which is true, and discard everything else.

While many think that the time of tribulation will kick off with a huge "bang," it is probably more likely that the world will gradually ease into that time period without many even realizing they are living in the final days. Remember, it will begin with a time of peace that is later followed by war, famine, and death as nations rise against nations. There will be an increase in the intensity and the frequency of natural disasters as God alerts His followers that the end is drawing near (Mt. 24:4–9). Those who are familiar with God's "Exit Strategy" will recognize what is happening, while others will just go about their normal routine unaware.

As things progress through this time of tribulation, Christians will be subjected to greater and greater persecution. There will be many who claim to be Christians who are not. When the heat gets turned up, and the price gets too high, they will quickly abandon their religion of convenience. In those days, the pretenders will be exposed for who they are, and many will walk away from the faith and betray those whose faith is genuine (Mt. 24:11).

Wickedness will increase, and the love of most will grow cold, but those who stand firm to the end will be saved (Mt. 24:13). Wickedness and deception will increase to the point that the lost world will follow a world leader who proclaims himself to be "God." His miracles and wonders will leave them convinced he is the one who holds the answers that their world needs. With the help of a false religious leader, he will attempt to force the world to acknowledge that he is the world's messiah. Those alive at this time will be required to choose between worshiping this new world leader, or refusing to worship him and being put to death. True Christians will refuse to bow to this individual and many will be martyred for their faith in Christ (Rev. 13:11–17).

During this time of great persecution, the boldness, strength, and conviction through which believers proclaim the gospel will be used by God to draw the final group of individuals to faith in Christ while it also hardens the hearts of those who will never repent. There will be no middle ground on which to stand. Believers will gain courage and boldness from knowing that Satan cannot take their lives until God's mission for their lives is complete. Even then, they will die with the assurance that in a very short time God will raise them up in full sight of those who have killed them (Rev. 11:7–12).

As all of these things unfold, God will be shaking the heavens and firing His final warning shots. There will be a tremendous spiritual battle that rages for the souls of men and women. The level of demonic activity will increase as many in the lost world are oppressed and possessed by Satan's fallen angels (demons). The distress of those days will be unlike anything the world has ever before seen (Mt. 24:21). The counterfeit miracles and signs will increase, fooling all who do not belong to Christ (Mt. 24:24).

As all of these things are taking place, the earth's ecosystem will be suffering through the terrible disasters described in the seals and trumpets. The earth will gradually become less and less inhabitable.

When the time comes, which God has set, and the harvest is fully ripe, Christ will break through the clouds and gather all those who belong to Him. The promise that Paul recorded will finally be fulfilled. It is the day all believers long for. Remember how Paul described that day? Listen, once again, to his words:

> *We believe that Jesus died and rose again and so we believe that God will bring with Jesus those who have fallen asleep in him. According to the Lord's own word, we tell you that we who are still alive, who are left till the coming of the Lord, will certainly not precede those who have fallen asleep. For the Lord himself will come down from heaven, with a loud command, with the voice of the archangel and with the trumpet call of God, and the dead in Christ will rise first. After that, we who are still alive and are left will be caught up together with them in the clouds to meet the Lord in the air. And so we will be with the Lord forever.* (1 Thess. 4:14–17)

Once Christ has returned, it will be too late for anyone else to repent and come to God for salvation. Their fate will have been sealed as Christ described in the parables He taught concerning His second coming (see Mt. 25).

Just as surely as all Christians will be gathered unto Christ, so also will all non-Christians be subjected to the terrible wrath of God. Following the removal of God's children, the terrible events described in the seven bowls of wrath will commence. The suffering will be unlike anything humanity has ever seen. Those who somehow manage to survive these events will be destroyed as Christ returns on His white horse with a sword in His mouth and His followers riding closely behind.

The antichrist and the false prophet will be captured and cast into the lake of fire, where they will spend their eternity. Satan will be bound and cast into the bottomless pit for a thousand years. During that period of time, Christ and His followers will reign over the demonic world. At the end of the thousand-year reign, Satan will be released for a short time to gather his demonic army for one final show-down with God. Fire will fall from Heaven and destroy them all. They will be cast into the lake of fire where the antichrist and false prophet were earlier sent.

Every human who has ever died without a personal relationship with Christ will be resurrected unto judgment. One by one, they will stand before God's Great White Throne where their sinfulness will be exposed and their lack of a relationship with God will be proven. They will then be cast into the lake of fire where they will forever remain.

Christians will be escorted into the place that God has prepared for them. He will dwell among them and will be their God, and they will be His people. For all of eternity they will share uninterrupted fellowship.

While this sounds almost too good to be true, it is absolutely true. The most amazing thing about God's "Exit Strategy" is that it will unfold exactly as He has described it. No matter how hard Satan may work to change the outcome, he is powerless to alter one part of the plan. God has always been, and will always remain completely sovereign. I hope you are ready for that great day!

PARTING THOUGHTS

NO ONE LEFT BEHIND

When I agreed to walk my friends through a study of the book of Revelation, I never dreamed it would lead to something like this. In fact, if I would have had any idea this is where things were headed I probably would have run for the door. For whatever reason, I believe that God had His hand in all the events that led me to put my discoveries on paper. I hope that even if you do not agree with everything that I have stated in this book that you will at least be stronger in your beliefs because you have searched the Scriptures for yourself.

It was my own search of the Scriptures that led me to the deep conviction that what I had been taught as a child was not in alignment with God's Word. To be honest, I liked what I was taught! It was comforting to think that as a believer in Christ I would be allowed to miss all of the suffering that will accompany the end. That sounded really enticing to me. However, when I searched the Scriptures for the proof that I needed to confirm those teachings, I did not find what I expected to find. Instead, I found what I have tried to pass on to you. At that point in the discovery process, I was faced with an incredibly important decision. I had to decide whether I would blindly accept what had been handed down to me and hope they were right, or dig deeper and deeper into God's Word to see for myself what God's Word revealed to be true. While this journey has been gut-wrenching at times, I believe it has been worth it for me. I hope this book has helped you to gain a better understanding of where this world is headed and what you need to do to prepare yourself, and those you love, for that day. More than anything in this world, I pray you will not be left behind when Christ returns.

If we were sitting across the table from one another, sharing what was foremost on our hearts, I would do everything possible to find a way to ask you this very personal question: "Friend, are you absolutely sure you are ready to meet God face to face?" You see, if the Bible makes one thing clear, it is this: we will all meet God face to face one day, either as our Savior or as our Judge. What we do with Jesus between now and then will determine whether we will experience the full measure of God's grace or the full measure of God's wrath.

I would ask, "Are you convinced in the depths of your heart that the relationship you profess to have with God is a genuine, life-changing, faith-based, grace-filled relationship?" If you were to reply that you were not absolutely sure, I would plead with you to do whatever it takes for you to gain that assurance.

I would share with you the truth of God's Word that reveals that every single one of us has sinned (Rom. 3:23). I would assure you that we all deserve to spend our eternity separated from the Living God because there is not one of us that is righteous or perfect (Rom. 3:10, 6:23a). I would then assure you that God offers us a way to avoid that tragic ending. There is a way back into a life-giving relationship with God through what Jesus did on the cross on our behalf (Rom. 6:23; Jn. 3:15–18), but the only way back is through faith in Jesus Christ (Jn. 14:1–6). I would remind you of God's promise to forgive us of our sins if we will turn from them to Him in repentance (1 Jn. 1:9). I would then urge you to make that decision right away. Do not put it off, or to give Satan another opportunity to deceive you one day longer. Finally, I would remind you of what Jesus said at the conclusion of the book of Revelation: *"I am coming soon and my reward is with me"* (Rev. 22:12).

Too much is at stake for you to postpone your decision. Now is the day of salvation. Now is the time for you to choose whom you will live the rest of your life for. I would pray that you would make the decision to enter into a personal relationship with God immediately.

Perhaps you would admit you feel the tugging of God at your heart, and perhaps you would indicate that you were ready to cross the line and commit your life to God's keeping. If you were to ask me how to do that, I would encourage you to yield your heart to God. Admit that you are a sinner, deserving of Hell. Believe in your heart that Jesus died in your place on the cross, and that He was resurrected three days later. Then, I would encourage you to invite Christ to take complete control of your life, to place His Holy Spirit inside of you, and to guide every step of your life from that moment on.

If you were to make your decision known to me, I would remind you of the great celebration that occurs throughout Heaven when a person turns his life over to God (Lk. 15:7). I would then say to you, "Welcome to the Family of God!" Then, with a huge grin on my face, and in my slow, Southern drawl I would say, "How 'bout us becoming neighbors when we get to Heaven?" I think I would like that a lot!

Friend, I may never get to have that face-to-face conversation with you, but I do wish that you would take this book, pour two cups of coffee, and pretend we were having it right now. Would you be able to look me in the eye and tell me that you are absolutely confident that your relationship with God is genuine? If not, why not get out your Bible and locate the verses I have listed above and try to understand exactly how much God has done in order for you to have a personal relationship with Him. Surrender your life and your future to Him. It is the only way to live life. Jesus Himself said it this way: *"I have come that you might have life and have it more abundantly"* (Jn. 10:10). Isn't it time you started living the life God created you to live?

Once you know Him as your Lord and Savior, you need to grow in your faith so that you will be able to stand when the tough times come. Seek God daily. Search His Word for the truth that you need in order to build a rock-solid faith. Immerse yourself in a local church that not only teaches the Word of God, but also encourages its members to live out the Word of God. Surround yourself with other believers who are passionately following God, and encourage them as they encourage you.

Finally, I would be so honored if you would let me know of your decision to follow Christ. I promise not to bombard you with tons of stuff, but I would like to pray for you as you live out your faith each day before a watching world. I hope to be writing other materials to assist new believers in their walk with God. If you are interested, I would be happy to notify you when they become available. You can contact me at: ExitStrategy@ImpactEternityNow.org. May God bless you as you seek after Him and Him alone!

We are now one day closer to the day that God executes His "Exit Strategy." I hope you are ready and waiting because our day of redemption is drawing near! (Lk. 21:28). As one good soldier would do for another, let's do all we can to make sure no one we know is left behind! Until we meet again . . .

FOR FURTHER STUDY

OTHER WORKS CONSULTED

The resources listed below are the ones I consulted as I did my research for this book. I am not endorsing any of them, but simply listing them for you to have in case you want to dig a little bit deeper into this subject. Some support my position, some contradict it, all helped sharpen it.

Armerding, Carl E. *The Olivet Discourse of Matthew 24-25 and other Studies.* Findley, Ohio: Dunham Press, n.d.

Aune, David E. *Word Biblical Commentary: Revelation 6-16.* Nashville: Thomas Nelson Publishing, 1995.

Barclay, William. *The New Daily Study Bible: The Revelation of John, Vol. 1.* Louisville, KY: Westminister John Knox Press, 2004.

_____. *The New Daily Study Bible: The Revelation of John, Vol. 2.* Louisville, KY: Westminister John Knox Press, 2004.

Berkhof, Louis. *Systematic Theology.* Grand Rapids: Eerdmans, 1938.

Blomberg, Craig L. *The New American Commentary: Matthew.* Nashville: Broadman Press, 1992.

Blomberg, Craig L. and Sung Wook Chung. *A Case for Historic Premillennialism: An Alternative to "Left Behind" Eschatology.* Grand Rapids: Baker Academic, 2009.

Boyce, James P. *Abstract of Systematic Theology.* Cape Coral, FL: Founders Press, 1971.

Brooks, James A. *The New American Commentary, Mark.* Nashville: Broadman Press, 1991.

Bruce, F. F. *Word Biblical Commentary: 1&2 Thessalonians.* Dallas, TX: Word Books, 1982.

Clouse, Robert G. *The Meaning of the New Millennium: Four Views.* Downers Grove, IL: InterVarsity Press, 1977.

_____. *The New Millennium Manual: A Once and Future Guide.* Grand Rapids: Baker Books, 1999.

Cooper, Lamar Eugene, Sr. *The New American Commentary: Ezekiel.* Nashville: Broadman and Holman Publishers, 1994.

Davis, Christopher A. *The College Press NIV Commentary: Revelation.* Joplin, MO: College Press Publishing Company, 2000.

Duty, Guy. *Escape From the Coming Tribulation: How To Be Prepared for the Last Great Crisis of History.* Minneapolis: Bethany Fellowship, 1975.

Easley, Kendall H. *Holman New Testament Commentary: Revelation.* Nashville: Holman Reference, 1988.

Eddleman, H. Leo. *The Second Coming.* Nashville: Broadman Publishers, 1963.

English, E. Schuyler. *Re-Thinking the Rapture: An Examination of What the Scriptures Teach as to the Time of the Translation of the Church in Relation to the Tribulation.* Neptune, NJ: Loizeaux Bros., 1954.

Erickson, Millard J. *A Basic Guide to Eschatology: Making Sense of the Millennium.* Grand Rapids: Baker Book House, 1998.

_____. *Christian Theology, Second Ed.* Grand Rapids: Baker Books, 1998.

_____. *Contemporary Options in Eschatology: A Study of the Millennium.* Grand Rapids, Baker Book House, 1998.

Evans, Craig A. *Word Biblical Commentary: mark 8:27–16:20.* Nashville: Thomas Nelson Publishers, 2001.

Ford, Desmond. *The Abomination of Desolation in Biblical Eschatology.* University Press of America, 1979.

Garrett, James Leo, Jr. *Systematic Theology: Biblical, Historical, and Evangelical, vol. 1, second ed.* Grand Rapids: Eerdmans, 1995.

_____. *Systematic Theology: Biblical, Historical, and Evangelical, vol. 2, second ed.* North Richland Hills, TX: BIBAL Press, 2001.

Grenz, Stanley J. *The Millennial Maze: Sorting Out Evangelical Options.* Downers Grove, IL: InterVarsity Press, 1992.

Grudem, Wayne. *Systematic Theology: An Introduction to Biblical Doctrine.* Grand Rapids: Zondervan, 1994.

Guelich, Robert A. *Word Biblical Commentary: Mark 1-8:26.* Dallas, TX: Word Books, 1989.

Gundry, Stanley N. ed. *Three Views on the Rapture: Pre-, Mid-, Or Post-tribulation.* Grand Rapids: Zondervan, 1996.

Hagner, Donald A. *Word Biblical Commentary: Matthew 1–13.* Dallas, TX: Word Books, 1993.

_____. *Word Biblical Commentary: Matthew 14–28.* Dallas, TX: Word Books, 1995.

Haldeman, I. M. *The Coming of Christ: Pre-Millennial and Imminent.* Charles Cook Publishers, 1906.

Harrison, Norman B. *The End: Re-Thinking the Revelation.* Minneapolis: Harrison Service, 1948.

Henry, Matthew. *Matthew Henry's Commentary on the Whole Bible, vol. 6, Acts to Revelation.* Hendrickson Publishers, 1991.

Hodge, Charles. *Systematic Theology, Vol. I.* Peabody, MA: Hendrickson Publishers, 2008.

_____. *Systematic Theology, Vol. II.* Peabody, MA: Hendrickson Publishers, 2008.

_____. *Systematic Theology, Vol. III.* Peabody, MA: Hendrickson Publishers, 2008.

Hoekema, Anthony. *The Bible and the Future.* Grand Rapids: Eerdmans, 1977.

Huey, F.B., Jr. *The New American Commentary, Jeremiah, Lamentations.* Nashville: Broadman Press, 1993.

Ice, Thomas and Timothy Demy, eds. *When the Trumpet Sounds.* Eugene, OR: Harvest House Publishers, 1995.

Ironside, Henry A. *Not Wrath But Rapture.* Neptune, NJ: Loizeaux Bros., 1989.

_____. *Romans, Ironside Commentaries.* Neptune, NJ: Loizeaux, 1998.

Katterjohn, Arthur D. *The Tribulation People.* Carol Stream, IL: Creation House, 1975.

Konig: Adrio. *The Eclipse of Christ in Eschatology: Toward a Christ-Centered Approach.* Grand Rapids: Eerdmans, 1989.

Ladd, George. *The Blessed Hope.* Grand Rapids: Eerdmans Publishing, 1956.

MacArthur, John Jr. *The MacArthur New Testament Commentary: Romans 1–8.* Chicago: Moody Press, 1991.

_____. *The MacArthur New Testament Commentary: Romans 9–16.* Chicago: Moody Press, 1994.

_____. *The MacArthur New Testament Commentary: (Digital Version on Computer).*

MacPherson, Dave. *The Incredible Cover-Up: The True Story on the Pre-Trib Rapture.* Plainfield, NJ: Logos International, 1975.

Martin, D. Michael. *The New American Commentary: 1, 2 Thessalonians.* Nashville: Broadman and Holman Publishers, 1995.

Mauro, Philip. *The Seventy Weeks and the Great Tribulation: A Study of the Last Two Visions of Daniel, and the Olivet Discourse of the Lord Jesus Christ.* Boston: Hamilton Bros., 1923.

McKeever, Jim. *Christians Will Go Through the Tribulation: And How to Prepare for It.* Medford, OR: Omega Publications, 1980.

Miller, Stephen R. *The New American Commentary, Daniel.* Nashville: Broadman and Holman Publishers, 1994.

Murray, George L. *Millennial Studies . . . A Search for Truth.* Grand Rapids: Baker Book House, 1948.

Nolland, John. *Word Biblical Commentary: Luke 1-9:20.* Dallas, TX: Word Books, 1989.

_____. *Word Biblical Commentary: Luke 18:35-24:53.* Dallas, TX: Word Books, 1991.

Packer, J. I. *Concise Theology: A Guide to Historic Christian Beliefs.* Carol Stream, IL: Tyndale House Publisher, 1993.

Phillips, John. *Exploring Revelation: An Expository Commentary.* Grand Rapids: Kregel Publications, 2004.

Reiter, Richard R. *The Rapture: Pre-, Mid-, Post-Tribulational?* Grand Rapids: Academic Books, 1984.

Robertson, Archibald Thomas. *Word Pictures in the New Testament, Vol. 1.* Nashville: Broadman Press, 1960.

_____. *Word Pictures in the New Testament, Vol. IV.* Nashville: Broadman Press, 1960.

Russell, J. Stewart. *The Parousia.* Grand Rapids: Baker Books, 1999.

Ryrie, Charles C. *Basic Theology: A Popular Systematic Guide to Understanding Biblical Truth.* Chicago: Moody Press, 1999.

Showers, Renald E. *The Pre-Wrath Rapture View: An Examination and Critique.* Grand Rapids: Kregel Publications, 2001.

Stein, Robert H. *The New American Commentary, Luke.* Nashville: Broadman Press, 1992.

Stewart, Leon O. *Too Late! The Truth About the Rapture, Tribulation, and Armageddon.* 2000.

Strong, Augustus H. *Systematic Theology.* Valley Forge, PA: Judson Press, 1907.

Tucker, Bruce. *The Posttribulational Rapture of the Church: With an Examination of the Theology of the Pretribulational Rapture of the Church.* Bridgewater, NJ: Replica Books, 2001.

Walvoord, John F. *The Blessed Hope and the Tribulation: A Biblical and Historical Study of Posttribulationism.* Grand Rapids: Zondervan Publishing House, 1976.

Warfield, Benjamin B. *Biblical and Theological Studies.* Philadelphia: The Presbyterian and Reformed Publishing Company, 1968.

www.ingramcontent.com/pod-product-compliance
Lightning Source LLC
La Vergne TN
LVHW090941080826
845145LV00003B/841

* 9 7 8 1 9 3 6 0 7 6 8 7 1 *